The Peace Prophecy

For Parker,

Peace + Love,

Elaine Christine

VISION 2013

Elaine Christine

The publisher offers discounts on this book when ordered in quantity for special sales. For more information, please contact:

AquaTerra
P.O. Box 410916
Melbourne, Florida 32941-0916
Phone: 321.449.8877
info@thepeaceprophecy.com

Editor: Dawn Schnuck
Author photograph: Damon Kappell, Studio 16
Cover design: Archer Ellison, Inc. Art Director Kimberly Leonard, and her staff at www.bookcovers.com, Lake Mary, FL 32795

Printed in the United States of America: All Service Graphics, Melbourne, FL 32935. Toll free: 888.775.0145

Library DDC: 299.93
Christine, Elaine M. 1957–
        The peace prophecy: vision 2013 / Elaine M. Christine.
        ISBN 978-0-9802030-0-4
CIP data is available from the Library of Congress.

ISBN 978-0-9802030-0-4

First printing, April 2009

DEDICATION

She was a fairly pragmatic person who gravitated more to concrete rather than spiritual approaches to life. And so, after she had read a few chapters from *The Peace Prophecy*, Heidi Robertson asked me, "Do you have to believe in Jesus?"

"No," I replied thoughtfully. "You can believe in love." This book is dedicated to my dear readers—may your hearts hold the grace of God, the forgiveness of Jesus Christ, and the comfort of the Holy Spirit—and that is love.

CONTENTS

FOREWORD:
PEACE PROCESS VALUED

Three years after my *Peace Process* session, I reviewed the transcript with Christine. I had come to closure with my deceased father, resolving my childhood issue of abandonment. And, my friend Ray, who I felt ignored me and didn't give me the attention I needed, moved out of my life. Those same feelings of being pushed aside continue with my son, Brian. Recently, I've made a choice to cut those cords and let him go with love. I'm going to love myself enough to let him go. The truth is, I don't want to write the story for my son. So, I'm giving him up to God.

I don't want to have regrets when I go to my grave. But, releasing negative habits is like losing a part of your body. Now there is an open wound—a void that has to fill up. The big hole is an opportunity to fill with love that unhealthy part of you that tried to prove you weren't lovable. I'm really learning what true love is, because my parents didn't teach me that.

When I read my transcript, I wondered. Do we actually want to change? You know, change is a choice. And, how can I change? The truth is, I still feel that I *need* to love me. But I want to come to a point where I *choose* to love me—it really is all about choice. When my thought patterns change, I know my situation will change. It has taken me three years, but better late than never—and, now I'm laughing about it!

After going through the *Peace Process*, I was able to identify unresolved childhood issues with my sister. I see our old drama manifesting in relationships with my female friends, so I'm working through releasing those negative patterns. I'm taking a closer look at the motive for my actions and I ask myself—am I self-serving or selfless and serving?

I am realizing the value of my *Peace Process* session. I've changed some of my negative thought patterns to new habits of love by being around nature, loving myself, and silently praying for the helpless child within me that I wanted to fix in others. When I remember to do these things, my life is beautiful, peaceful, and harmonious. It's simple. You can do the same thing over and over again, but, when you're ready, do the *Peace Process*—it works.

Rev. Audrice Collins
Melbourne Beach, Florida

ACKNOWLEDGEMENTS

In my dream, I spoke with a woman who told me what to leave in the book and what to take out. That female voice is none other than my dear friend and editor, Dawn Schnuck. Thank you, Dawn—our friendship is a treasure woven into the pages of *The Peace Prophecy*. When I told my husband, Tom, that I was going to Yoga College for nine weeks in California, his immediate response was "No, you're not!" Ten years later, Tom has proved to be the greatest supporter of my transformation from caterpillar to butterfly. Thank you, Tom— your patience and generosity are keynotes of our beautiful marriage.

I wish to acknowledge my family, especially June, Ryan, and Erika for teaching me how to be a better step-mom, and all those who helped through my caterpillar stage of growth, which is characterized by feeding, survival, and preparation for the next phase. James Redfield, author of *The Celestine Prophecy*, fed his readers with a vision of life lived as a spiritual adventure. Thank you, James—after I read your book, I began to see synchronicities, trust inner guidance, and follow my spiritual path.

My preparation included completing *A Course in Miracles* workbook and meeting with Ken Wapnick at the Foundation for A Course in Miracles. Thank you, Ken—you are an inspiration for tirelessly teaching inner peace based on the miracles of love and principles of forgiveness. It was Marshall Govindan who taught me Babaji's Kriya Yoga: unity in diversity, world peace, and God-realization. Thank you, Marshall—your pilgrimage to sacred sites in India and hike in the Himalayas was a most exciting journey!

I was an elder in a Presbyterian Church writing the *Good News* when God called me to form my chrysalis within the cocoon at *Yoga with Christine*. My gratitude extends to Linda Sands, my DreamQuest teacher, for guiding me to connect with my heart's desire. Thank you, Linda—for the enchanting evening when we shared a commitment to the divine feminine. They say when the student is ready, the teacher will appear—and Al Rapaport showed up to teach Zen meditation. Thank you, Al—I owe my joy of sitting and deep breathing to you!

For three years I studied and practiced *The Way of Mastery* by Jon Marc Hammer. Thank you, Jayem—your pilgrimage to sacred sites in Israel was an unforgettable and uplifting experience. My angel portrait is a blessing painted by artist extraordinaire Glenda Green. Thank you, Glenda—she is so lovely and serves as a reminder to emerge and bring *peace to every mind*.

Elaine Marie Christine
Merritt Island, Florida

ABOUT THE AUTHOR

Elaine M. Christine wrote a process for world peace in 1998, after her text *Managing Risk: Methods for Software Systems Development* was published. She had a vision of the peace symbol while walking the beach in Indialantic, Florida on the morning of August 5, 2000. For the next eight years, she wrote more than 57 inches of material in 19 binders known as *The Christine Revelation*. Christine founded AquaTerra in 2005 with the mission *Peace to Every Mind*®. Dedicated to uplifting humanity to the new Peace Consciousness, Christine trains, certifies, and mentors *Peace Process* facilitators. Visit Dr. Christine online at www.thepeaceprophecy.com.

The Peace Prophecy

PART I

Peace Visionary

And the temple of God was opened in heaven.

—Revelation [11:19]

Part I describes a spiritual vision that I experienced in the year 2000. The cosmic knowledge revealed to me was profound. Unable to speak of the emotional experience, I began to write. The following year, I was guided to open a yoga studio on Fifth Avenue in Indialantic, Florida. I wanted to name my new spiritual sandbox Oasis, but a still, small voice said, "The planet is the Oasis—you are *Yoga with Christine*."

Chapter 1, **A Home-Coming**. This chapter shows how forgiveness became the key to freeing my subconscious from isolation, revealing the embrace of a higher consciousness. My vision of peace on August 5, 2000 is significant as 8 + 5 + 2000 adds to 2013, pointing to the time humanity awakens to its true nature.

Chapter 2, **New Day for Dawn**. Dawn seeks spiritual growth and we meet at *Yoga with Christine*. Our mutual friends knew me as Dr. Elaine Hall, software process improvement consultant and author of *Managing Risk*, and believe I have lost my marbles to give up a lucrative career. Despite the community chatter and friends who are resistant to my change, I recreate myself, emerging as Christine.

1

A Home-Coming

She came home at high tide
Under the cloud of night,
Seeking the shore of her birth,
Her predestination in the moonlight.

I wasn't privileged to see her,
But her tracks told me her story,
Of her search to find just the right
Place for her moment of glory.

—Shirley Evelyn Price Pekar

"Want me to move the car?" It was 8:00 AM and I sensed that Tom was ready for work. Tom's love of cars led to our ritual of moving all four of them around, as our garage had room for two. The garage, the driveway, and the mini-storage alternately held the Big Benz, the Blue Car, the 930, and the 560.

"I can do it." Tom jingled his keys. "The storage garage closes at noon. I'll call you then."

"I'm going to the beach," I said, giving him a kiss goodbye.

1.1   ON THE EDGE OF CONSCIOUSNESS

It was a twenty-minute trek to the Indialantic public beach. As I walked, my mind drifted to the past month of activity. Hmm, it's August 5, 2000 today and it seems that inspiration began to flood my awareness within the last week. What had triggered it? Perhaps it was the hug I gave to my stepson, my hidden hates and secret sins finally conquered by a genuine embrace. The experience of forgiveness was the proof necessary to convince my subconscious that I had accepted forgiveness for myself. Maybe it helped that I facilitated the recent group meeting for *A Course in Miracles*.

It had been an exciting, exhausting week. There were many late nights well after 3:00 AM, and a few afternoon naps. I was grateful—I had tapped into something special. Perhaps I called it to myself with my questions. I crossed A1A and took the Grosse Pointe beach access between two condos, one white and one yellow. At the top of the stairs, I looked down to note the two sets of stairs that led to the beach. *Three levels*, I mused. My mind wandered as I descended the steps, counting from one to seven. At the next level, I began to count again.

The sun was bright and warm, and it was low tide. *Plenty of sand to walk on*, I thought. As I walked, I noticed the ocean waves coming onto shore. Gentle waves washed the beach at the shoreline, covering the sand. I watched the salty water sink deep into the sand. *Consciousness is like that*, I thought. *The super conscious is the water that covers the sand, our conscious mind. Our subconscious must be the wet feel of the sand as the water sinks beneath it. We become aware of the super conscious only after it goes below our conscious awareness.* The analogy was particularly helpful, so I silently said a blessing to God or whoever had just shared the thought with me.

1.2 MILLENNIUM PEACE VISION

On my way, a girl ran past. I smiled at her, noticing she had a pretty face and hefty body. She smiled in return. I walked by a black man, several white men, and a woman fishing with long poles in the surf. It seemed no one was having any luck. At the south end of the Indialantic public beach, I turned around. The same pony-tailed girl ran toward me in the opposite direction. This time I spoke as I smiled, "Good morning."

"Water," I heard her say, thinking that she must be breathlessly trying to communicate the beauty of the Atlantic Ocean.

Then I saw her gazing at the water bottle, clenched firmly in my hand. With the realization that she was thirsty and not admiring the scenery, I extended my arm and offered, "Would you like some? There is plenty here."

"No, that's okay, but thanks, anyway. Have a nice day."

"You too!" Her face brightened as I turned back to continue my journey.

I love the beach. There is something wonderful about walking on the beach. I felt great, not overly excited because I was tired from walking, and still waking up. I just felt happy, with a smile on my face. I felt peaceful. That's when I saw a vision of the peace symbol as a neon-violet color projected from my mind's eye. The revelation I had recently that the Circle of Fifths in music was both the solar cycle, and with God's step, the lunar cycle—was now mapped onto a glowing peace symbol! Just for a moment, I gazed in amazement. Gratitude filled my heart as I gave thanks for the awareness of how perfectly the puzzle fit together.

That's when it hit me. *The peace symbol was the missing piece of the Six-Discipline Model.* I burst into tears as the wave of knowledge washed over me and sank to the level of my awareness. I cried because I saw the Six-Discipline Model that Tom and I developed came from a selfish human perspective. The lack of symmetry that Tom had complained about, which I thought was the hindbrain, performing low-level functions, was made whole by the peace symbol. I cried because it was so beautiful. My nose ran and I couldn't resist lifting my T-shirt and blowing so I could breathe again. I didn't care if anyone saw my bra, or if my T-shirt had snot on it.

1.3 BIRTH OF ONE THOUSAND TURTLES

Close to the condos, a man and two young boys were watching their feet—no, something moving on the sand. Baby loggerhead turtles! I could feel their excitement as I approached them.

"How about that?" the man said, "There must be a thousand of them!"

"Aren't they cute?" I asked the boys. They nodded in agreement. "That is very special to see, isn't it?" I hoped the boys would appreciate that this was not an everyday occurrence.

The man continued, "I thought they came out at night, but maybe the sun looks about like the moon right now."

"I think it is around 9 AM. What time is it?" I inquired, noticing that the man wore a wristwatch.

"Eight-thirty four," he read from his digital watch.

"Well, I have seen turtles laying their eggs, but I have never seen them hatch." I offered my limited knowledge of turtle reproduction. "But, one time when I was scuba diving, I came around a ledge and met a huge turtle face-to-face. She had a head the size of yours," I motioned to the older boy.

As we gazed in amazement, the baby turtles began to take different paths to reach the ocean. "They are coming from that nest. We've been watching them come out," the man said.

"Let's have a look." I was eager to see turtles hatching. The sand moved and one little head was visible in the shifting sand. Then another head appeared, as if twins were coming. The flipper of the first appeared stuck to the head of the second, but they separated and went their own way—over the ripples, up the sand mountain and down again. One struggled on its back after tumbling down, but quickly recovered as the earnest fins kept flapping.

A couple approached and the woman said to her husband, "Oh, we left the camera in the car—we should go and get it."

"Have you ever seen this before?" I asked, intuiting what the answer from these tourists would be.

"No, we just moved here from Kentucky. We've come to the beach for the volleyball game."

"Oh, that's nice," I offered with enthusiasm for their new start. "We're all from Indialantic," I indicated for the boys, their father, and myself.

"The birds already got one of the babies," the father turned to me and confided. "Do you see those birds out there?" He pointed to three low-flying pelicans in formation.

I nodded. "They are going to tell their friends—and I suppose that is part of it." I smiled, knowing that birds eat as surely as turtles are born. I followed a tiny turtle to the water where his fins made a clear path—right, left, right, left in the wet sand. The next wave crashed on the shore, pushing the turtle back, sweeping him off his feet, where the undertow dragged him down. *He was home.*

1.4   A GARDEN IN THE SAND

As I turned to head home myself, I began to cry again. Not for the turtles, but for my own life experience. I remembered that my mother had written a poem about turtles. Part of the poem was written up in an article about her in the Palm Beach Post. She had built a three-tier garden in the sand on Delray Beach behind my grandparents' estate, where the large loggerhead turtles nested in the moonlight. Her poetry was never published, although it was really quite good. I decided then that I would share a part of her poem to honor her memory.

I entered the modest home I had lived in for eighteen years and took off my shoes. In the kitchen, the clock on the microwave read 9:00 AM. Tears stained my cheeks and I wore the soiled T-shirt as I walked into my office, sat down at the computer, and began to type.

1.5   EXERCISE

1.   Forgive those who trespass against you:

   a.   List the people who irritate you. You know the ones that get under your skin? Write down their names as well as the behaviors that really bug you.

   b.   How can you show forgiveness? For each person on your list, jot down something nice that you could do.

   c.   Accept forgiveness for yourself by saying with all of your heart: I love you. God bless you. Please forgive me!

2.   Share your experiences of nature and with individuals that have profoundly moved or inspired you.

3.   Just as the tide ebbs and flows, your unique path has ups and downs. Identify the ways your life reflects this natural cycle.

2

New Day for Dawn

Daylight
I must wait for the sunrise
I must think of a new life
And I mustn't give in.

When the dawn comes
Tonight will be a memory too,
And a new day will begin.

—Andrew Lloyd Webber

This summer I wake about 6:00 AM, just as the sun begins to paint its colors across the brightening sky. What with exercising several mornings a week, a little part-time business and some volunteer work, the days race by. Going to bed to read or to listen to an audio program at 9:00 PM seems a welcome retreat. Of course, I fall asleep after only a few pages.

Lately, with the years accumulating so rapidly, I ponder making an effort to extend my waking hours. I know I haven't

13

finished what I'm here on earth to do. And who knows how much time is left?

At 8:45 AM several Thursdays ago, with that thought in mind, I decided to stop at the new place I'd discovered on Fifth Avenue in Indialantic. I had just completed a full workout routine at the gym when it occurred to me that maybe an evening class with a spiritual component would inspire my personal clock to expand.

2.1   YOGA WITH CHRISTINE

I park behind the building, sitting a few moments in my car trying to decide if I really want to complicate my schedule. After all, I am very grateful for a generous amount of freedom. A classic Mercedes convertible pulls up beside my car and a dark-haired young woman smiles in my direction. I watch as she enters the door that advertises "Yoga with Christine."

Oh well, I'm here, I reassure myself. *At least I can ask what's going on.*

The woman I had seen greets me at the door. "Hi," she said. "I'm Christine."

"Oh!" I am surprised to find myself face-to-face with someone in whose interest it might be to sell me something. I consider backing out. I want to look, but I am not prepared to buy.

But she smiles in such a genuine and friendly way—and it is just the two of us—so I answer, "Well, hello, Christine. My name is Dawn."

"Dawn! What a pretty name!" She holds out her hand.

"Oh, thanks! I noticed your sign and thought I'd have a look at what you're doing here," I confess.

Her face becomes animated as she tells me, "Hatha yoga in the mornings and evenings, Dance your Spirit on Monday nights, and a discussion group about *A Course in Miracles*, and oh, as time goes by we will offer more and more exciting things." Her face glows with enthusiasm.

"Wow! *A Course in Miracles* . . . that's interesting," I respond. I know a little about the *Course* after years of listening to Marianne Williamson.

"Uh! And, I forgot the writing group! I'm a published author and we have a writing group that meets here once a month," she continues, breathless.

A writing group. Wow! Writing has been my creative expression for many years.

"Come on in. Let me show you around," she offers, turning toward the large room beyond. I follow her. Comfortably carpeted in a dark green with several bright posters hanging about, the space appears serene and welcoming. Mirrors cover one entire wall with two dolphins, one on each end, etched in the glass. Christine stoops over a small fountain to turn it on. Soon, soothing sounds fill the background as water emerges from the top of a patina pineapple.

"Have you ever considered yoga?" Christine asks.

I pause. "Well, actually, not recently. I mean, I've thought about it a couple of times in my life but never really looked into it.

Right now, I go to the gym weekday mornings. As a matter of fact, I just came from there," I tell her, sweeping my hand in front of my bicycle shorts and oversized T-shirt as further explanation.

"Ah," she nods. "Well, yoga is good."

I can see that. She is tiny and slim.

"So, to help you as you're thinking about this, why don't you choose a card from this deck? Each card contains a thought—an idea, from *A Course in Miracles*—and, if nothing else, you can take that idea home with you as a—a point of contemplation." She reaches for a small basket and passes it to me. I select a card and hand it back to her.

"You may be shown the path to wisdom—but only you can take the first step . . ." she reads. She looks up at me, her face a question.

I chuckle. "Well, that could be a message for me, couldn't it? I'll tell you what. I will think about it, Christine."

"That's perfect," she laughs, extending her hand again.

I turn to the door as three women walk in for the 9 o'clock class. Christine welcomes each one personally as I leave.

Hmm, I thought to myself. Yoga? *A Course in Miracles*? And a writing group! Well, maybe . . .

2.2   A CHANGE IN PERSPECTIVE

He's right on time, looking cool and tropical in an embroidered white Indian-style shirt. I give him a big hug. He is not cool, after

16

all, but sweaty—it's a hot walk to our condo from his. He removes his handkerchief to wipe his head as my husband Bob pours him a tall goblet of cold white wine. The two of them sit on stools at the counter looking into the kitchen and attack the softened brie and Carr's crackers. I, glass of red wine nearby, continue with dinner prep on the other side.

"What do you hear from Flo?" I ask eagerly. We have invited Vic for dinner while his wife Flo is in London studying American and British perspectives on the War of Independence. After a week of that, she's off to Denmark to absorb the Danish use of windmills for energy—and its effects on farming there.

"Well, I get these one-liners a couple of times a day," Vic answers.

"Ah, so she's found a computer to use." I smile knowing that one of the first things Flo would find in London would be a computer for email to check in with Vic.

"Oh yes—it might be a little too handy," Vic responds wryly even as a pleased look plays across his face.

"Is she happy with the course material? Has she found any kindred spirits among the other students?" I am keen to hear how she is doing since I know she hoped to discuss her idea that the current Israeli/Palestinian situation might be a late-date parallel to the War of Independence—and other complicated theories she's devised.

"It's funny. She writes only a few words—and never any details," Vic rues. Of course, I know Flo as a prolific writer and can't imagine her skipping the meat.

2.3   INDEPENDENCE DAY

"I just think it is so great that she will do something like this. I mean, how many women do you know travel on their own to study something—anything? I am so impressed."

"Yeah, well, she's interested in all this odd-ball stuff." Vic grins. His view of his wife's enthusiasms is tolerant and good-natured, despite his words.

We go on to discuss the merits to men whose wives take off on separate endeavors.

"It's great when Dawn is gone for awhile," Bob puts in. "I can do anything I want . . ." and then he adds, "any time I want."

Vic agrees. "She gets a vacation and I get a vacation." He slathers another Carr's with brie. "What the hell do I care about windmills in Denmark?" Bob nods; we all laugh. Flo's interests are academic and very broad.

"How wonderful it must be for her to have the opportunity to be with others who share her passion for history," I offer. Flo often tries to educate me, all the while tsk-tsking about how I got to be so old without learning anything. "Don't you READ?" she once asked.

"Yeah, yeah," Vic agrees. "I'm sure she's like a pig in shit."

We chortle at this, knowing exactly what Vic means. Flo is a voracious student.

The brie is about gone and dinner is a few minutes away. I change the subject.

2.4   A BUTTERFLY EMERGES

"You know, Vic, I am taking this yoga class from a young woman you might know. Her name used to be Elaine something and her husband is a guy who works with your friend, Ron. Now she calls herself Christine." Ron is president of a local company and Vic is a member of Ron's board.

"What do you mean *her name used to be*?"

"Well, she's had a divorce and some personal stuff and I think she said she's starting again by changing her name. Really, I don't know that much about her yet."

Vic is thoughtful. "You don't mean Elaine Hall, do you?" he asks. "We know her well."

"Yeah! I think that was her name. She wrote a book on something . . ."

"She wrote a book on software. I read it." Vic is a computer whiz and software inventor so I press him for details.

He tosses off my question with another one. "What's this about her changing her name?"

"Uh, from what I understand, she's had a complete metamorphosis . . ."

"Metamorphosis?" Vic asks, his tone incredulous. "What about?"

It's hard to get a rise out of Vic, no matter what, so I pursue the topic with delight.

"It's just that now she's into yoga and other kinds of things like meditation—more spiritual stuff."

Bob and Vic have similar thoughts on this score. "You don't mean New Age, do you?"

"Yeah, I would say so," I reply proudly, being more than a little that way myself.

Vic puts his head in his hands. "Oh, my God, another good scientific mind gone to pot," he laments.

Bob lights the candles and I carry the plate of pork tenderloin to the table.

"Hey! New Age has got a lot of good stuff." I pass the rice.

"It's a bunch of nothing, that's what it is," Vic says as he hands the salad to Bob.

I don't want to push my luck with the New Age discussion— better to save it until I have a little more backup present—not that Vic or Bob will ever be convinced. But, it tickles me to bait Vic a bit—to see him roll his eyes and bury his head. And then, the conversation turns to other, more important issues—boats and their upkeep, classical music, and movies.

2.5   EXERCISE

1.   Describe your current passion and pursuits, recent studies, and/or new endeavors that are helping you to grow.

2.   List the kindred spirits or like-minded friends you have found to share your journey.

3.   Remember a time when you began again—perhaps with a new name, relationship, or career. How did you recreate yourself?

PART II

Peace to Every Mind

Peace of mind is clearly an internal matter.
It must begin with your own thoughts,
and then extend outward.
It is from your peace of mind that a
peaceful perception of the world arises.

—A Course in Miracles

Part II describes my teaching a two-hour interactive *Peace Process* workshop as I begin to fulfill the mission of *peace to every mind*. The workshop includes a breathing exercise to relax and focus the group. A word association game enables participants to create their own phrases defining the *Peace Process*. Individuals record confidential perceptions on a Peace Process Worksheet, which lists the six simple steps to inner peace. I explain the Six-Discipline Model of the individual mind and present the new Peace Consciousness as a model of a universal mind. I share my desire to teach the *Peace Process* as a path to psychological well-being.

Chapter 3, **Angel of Peace**. Retreat coordinator Darlene Capinha calls me to present the *Peace Process* to a group of Unity Church chaplains. The workshop begins with the Peace BEE breathing exercise to nourish the body with the breath of life. The chaplains play an interactive word association game and define the *Peace Process* for themselves by sharing words to make profound phrases.

Chapter 4, **Peace Process Worksheet**. The Unity chaplains take their personal issues through the *Peace Process* and make their own contributions to world peace. Each person records individual perceptions on the Peace Process Worksheet. Their information is confidential; sharing is voluntary.

Chapter 5, **The Blessed Hope**. Dr. Wanda Bethea visits me to learn how she can apply the *Peace Process* in her private counseling practice. I describe the Six-Discipline Model of the mind and my inspiration to write the thought of world peace. I present a new Peace Consciousness that joins an individual mind with *Energy* to create a universal mind. I tell my personal story and desire to teach the *Peace Process* and bring *peace to every mind.*

3

Angel of Peace

To have peace, teach peace to learn it.

—Helen Schucman

The phone rang. Christine glanced down at the cordless receiver. The caller ID display announced *Darlene Capinha*. Christine smiled. Darlene had been her friend for more than eight years. She eagerly picked up the phone. "Hello?" Christine said slowly, pretending not to know who was on the other line.

"Hi Christine, it's Darlene." There was a song in her voice as she spoke.

"Hi Darlene. How are you?" Christine was introduced to Darlene in the year 2000, when Darlene facilitated a study group for *A Course in Miracles*. Since that time, Darlene continued as facilitator of the group.

"I'm fine. Did you know that I am the coordinator for the next Unity chaplains' retreat?" Darlene began with a question.

"No, but that's great!" Christine encouraged.

"And, I prayed for a speaker that would be inspiring . . ." Darlene explained.

"Un-huh." Christine listened intently.

"So, I woke up this morning and heard—*call Christine to do the Peace Process*," Darlene said.

"Well, thank you, Darlene." Christine smiled. "I'd love to do that." She knew this was not a paid assignment, but that never mattered. Christine went wherever she felt called to go.

"Oh, good! You'll have an hour and a half to present. I'll send you the presenters' schedule and directions to the Retreat Center," promised Darlene.

"And I will ask Mother Mary to preside over a committee of angels to help me prioritize the material." Christine had a simple method for inspiration. "I'll just work for them," she told Darlene.

3.1   AN ANGEL ARRIVES AT AQUATERRA

The following week, Audrice Collins arrived from Melbourne Beach at AquaTerra, Christine's home in Merritt Island. "Christine, did you read the newspaper article about my Angel Workshop?"

"No, I didn't see it." Christine shook her head as Audrice handed her the article cut from the newspaper. "That's a nice photo of you, Audrice."

"Do you think you could make a copy so I can send it to my son?" Audrice asked.

"Sure, I can. We'll scan it and email it to your family and friends," Christine offered.

"Thank you!" Audrice was excited to share her story. "I hear you are preparing for a workshop, so tell me about it." Audrice settled comfortably into the black leather chair in Christine's office.

Christine sat down on the silk pillow on the Oriental rug. "Darlene called from Unity of Melbourne to ask me to do a workshop at their chaplains' retreat. I'm planning to teach how to BEE Peace. After that, I think we'll do the word association for *Peace Process*. Then I'd like the group to take their personal issues through the *Peace Process* and make their own individual contributions to world peace."

"Be peace, what is that?" Audrice had been a teacher of the *Peace Process* for almost four years, but this was new to her.

"Picture a bee—and that is the acronym for *Breathe*, *Energize*, and *Embrace*. Peace BEE is a simple way to center the group," Christine explained. "I used these three breathing techniques when our tour bus in Italy was delayed. Many people who were irritated calmed down and several said they enjoyed the experience."

"So, what else are you going to do?" Audrice wanted to know.

"Maybe we could say the *Prayer of St. Francis* and invite him to join with us in spirit as we begin," Christine suggested.

"Don't you have a prayer of your own?" Audrice persisted.

"Well, yes—I wrote a poem about peace several years ago. It's somewhere on my computer. I'll look for it," Christine promised.

After enjoying lunch on the back patio, Audrice and Christine returned to the office to continue working together. When Audrice left AquaTerra late that afternoon, Christine said "Audrice, I know why you came over today. You have been a heavenly helper!"

3.2   A WORKSHOP FOR UNITY

On Saturday Tom drove Christine to the Canterbury Retreat Center in Oviedo, Florida. Christine was quiet as she stared out the window, her mind lost in thought. Suddenly, her eyes widened and her jaw dropped. *No! Impossible!* She turned her head quickly to be certain of what she saw. A large pink pig in the ditch—the pig was dead. *Oh, my!* She closed her mouth, wondering if she was imagining things. She glanced back at Tom, but his eyes were focused on the road ahead. "We're almost there," Tom announced as he turned onto Alafaya Trail.

Tom helped Christine set up for the workshop while the chaplains took their lunch break. He manned the video camera and turned on the voice recorder, attaching it to Christine's dress. The chaplains returned to the conference room—all, that is, except for Joan Lamb.

Darlene counted heads. "Where's Joan?" she asked, unable to disguise her irritation. It was time to begin.

To help with the introduction, Darlene requested a short bio from Christine. Instead of sending her biography, Christine asked Darlene to say a few words from her heart.

Darlene began with her heartfelt introduction. "It is my pleasure to present Dr. Christine. She's going to do her workshop on the *Peace Process* that she developed with spirit or spirit with her—however you want to say that—they were joined together as one during its development. Her husband Tom is going to videotape the workshop for future use. So, I'm happy to present Dr. Christine." The chaplains clapped politely as Darlene took her seat.

"Thank you, Darlene. And thanks to everyone for being here. I have been teaching the *Peace Process* for ten years now, so it is time to share it with a wider audience. I most often use the *Peace Process* as a one-on-one counseling tool. Today I'm going to take the group through the *Peace Process* and we're going to make a contribution to world peace."

"Yes!" Bonnie exclaimed, not being able to contain her enthusiasm and passion for peace.

3.3   BREATHE TO BE PEACEFUL

"It is important to remember that the breath controls consciousness. So, we're going to begin this workshop with a breathing exercise to center our minds and be peaceful. Please sit up straight in your chairs and put your pens down."

All the chaplains sat back in the blue-cushioned chairs, except for Janet. She leaned forward, eager to begin.

Christine gestured toward a colorful poster of a bee sitting on a pretty wildflower. "We're going to breathe with the Peace BEE. The acronym BEE stands for *Breathe, Energize,* and *Embrace,*" Christine explained.

"We'll take sixteen breaths using the thumb and four fingers on our non-dominant hand to count. Use your left hand if you are right-handed. If we have any lefties—I know Tom is a leftie—you can start with your right." Christine smiled as she glanced at Tom.

"Begin by putting your thumb and index finger together, placing the thumbnail to the tip of the nail on the index finger."

A woman with red hair walked into the room and sat down. "I hope that's Joan. Welcome back," Christine acknowledged. "We are centering ourselves with a breathing exercise. Joan, are you right-handed?" Joan nodded. "Then use your left hand and put the nail tips of your thumb and index finger together."

Christine continued. "Now, take a breath in through your nose to filter your air. Keep your mouth closed as you exhale, taking time to assimilate the oxygen. Then, move your thumb to the first pad on the index finger. Inhale, breathe in from your belly." Christine lifted her shoulders. "Exhale and relax." She slowly lowered her shoulders. "Move to the middle pad and inhale again— and exhale gently. Last pad on the index finger, inhale, and draw a deeper breath. Fill your lungs like party balloons. As you exhale, lower your shoulders away from the neck." Christine moved from table to table demonstrating the breathing exercise.

"Move your thumb to the middle finger. Nail to nail, inhale and you might imagine walking on the beach. Exhale. As you move your thumb to the first pad, breathe in. You may want to close your eyes now. Exhale slowly. Move your thumb to the middle pad, inhale—imagine a beautiful day and the sun shining down upon you. Exhale and relax. Move your thumb to the last pad of the middle finger and inhale from below the belly button. Feel your chest expand as you breathe in the salt-sea air. Let the warmth of the sun melt all your cares away, and exhale." Several chaplains closed their eyes.

"Now, your thumb moves to the ring finger, nail to nail. Inhale and breathe from your toes. Imagine feeling soft sand under your feet. Exhale an even, balanced breath. First pad, breathe in and say to yourself: one, two, three, and four. Exhale, one, two, three, and four. Move to the middle pad and inhale one, two, three, four, and five. Exhale, one, two, three, four, and five. Last pad, breathe in from your toes a longer, deeper breath. Exhale and envision a flock of birds flying overhead."

Christine continued. "Move your thumb to your pinky, nail to nail. Breathe in and listen for the sound of the ocean, and exhale—hear the waves washing onto shore. Inhale with the thumb on the first pad—one, two, three, four, and five. Exhale one, two, three, four, and five. With practice, your breath becomes stronger.

Middle pad, breathe in one, two, three, four, five, and six. Exhale, one, two, three, four, five, and six. Move your thumb to the last pad on the pinky, breathe in. Exhale—you are fresh and ready for the next session."

The conference room was quiet except for the sound of soft breathing.

"All right, you can open your eyes. That is the 'B' in BEE, which stands for *Breathe*." Christine's gaze spanned the group.

"The letter 'E' stands for *Energize*. Now, inhale and raise your right arm overhead. When the arm touches your ear, bend the elbow, placing your hand over the left ear. Take a breath and gently tilt your head to the right side, opening the major artery that allows fresh oxygen to energize the brain. Exhale and lower your hand."

Christine watched as tilted heads came slowly upright.

"Raise your left arm as you inhale and when your arm is overhead, bend the elbow and place your hand over the right ear. Breathe again and exhale, guiding your head to the left side. Feel open-minded, patient, and kind. Lower your hand, and we complete the first 'E' in BEE.

"The last 'E' is for *Embrace*. Wrap your arms around your shoulders and walk your fingers in an inch. Breathe deeply and give yourself a squeeze. Reclaim all those body parts that have ever failed you. Take another breath. Squeeze and reclaim all the parts that you said you didn't like. Take one more deep breath, and give yourself a big hug, knowing you are perfect just as you are, right now."

Christine smiled in her own self-acceptance. Some of the chaplains applauded.

"Being peaceful is a choice. Be gentle with yourself. Remember to *Breathe, Energize,* and *Embrace* with Peace BEE!"

3.4   *PEACE PROCESS* WORD ASSOCIATION

"Now, let's play a word association game." Christine clapped her hands and turned to face the flip chart. "At the top left side of the paper I will write *Peace*," she explained as she wrote with a purple marker. Turning back to the group, she asked them to think of words associated with peace. "If you can't think of a word, say 'pass' and we'll come back to you."

Christine turned to the first person on her left. "I say *Peace* and you say . . ."

"Source energy." Sally was quick to respond.

"Source energy," Christine repeated as she wrote on the left side of the flip chart. "Thank you, Sally."

"I say *Peace* and you say . . ." Christine addressed the next woman.

"Love," Bonnie said softly.

"Love," Christine nodded. She turned to the chaplain sitting beside Bonnie.

"Calm," suggested Ros.

"Calm." Christine scribbled.

"Harmony," Grace said.

33

Christine jotted on the paper. "Thank you, Grace. And, Dave?"

"Trust," Dave said with authority.

"Trust." Christine added to the list.

"God," said Dixie with conviction.

Christine wrote the word and then turned to Joan Lamb.

"Still," Joan said quietly.

"Still." Christine scrawled. She looked at Gary.

"Creative," Gary contributed without a prompt.

"Thank you. Okay, Janet?"

"Balanced," Janet shared.

Christine nodded. "Sonja?"

"Gift." Sonja offered.

Christine wrote the word close to the bottom of the flip chart.

"Do we have room for a word from Darlene?" Christine winked at the group.

"Yes!" Several chaplains exclaimed in unison.

"Oh, okay!" Christine laughed. With a big smile, she faced her teacher of *A Course in Miracles*. "What do you think, Darlene?"

"Unlimited." Darlene shared.

"Unlimited!" Christine repeated. "Well, I'm glad we included you," she teased as she turned to write the last word.

3.5   THE JOY OF CREATION

"We're not done," Christine cautioned the group. "We're just getting started! At the top right side of the paper I will write *Process*," she explained as she penned the word with a dark blue marker."

Christine turned to the person on her left. "I say *Process* and you say . . ."

"Creation." Sally was quick to answer.

Christine wrote on the right side of the flip chart.

"Bonnie?" Christine asked.

"Joy," Bonnie contributed.

"Joy," Christine repeated. She turned to Ros.

"Steps," contributed Ros.

Christine saw that the group was thinking as a cohesive unit. They moved quickly without a prompt.

"Laughter," Grace offered.

"Thank you, Grace." Christine jotted. She turned around. "Dave?"

"Teaching," Dave said with confidence.

Christine nodded.

"Meditate," said Dixie.

"Okay, I got it," Christine confirmed.

"Function," Joan said.

Gary said, "Action."

"Thank you." Christine tilted her head toward Janet.

"Be in the moment," Janet added.

"Sonja?" Christine turned toward her.

"Divine order," Sonja shared.

Christine wrote her words close to the bottom of the flip chart.

Christine waited for an input from Darlene.

"Being," Darlene said reverently.

"Being," Christine repeated as she scrawled.

The page was full. Christine stepped aside and said, "Can everyone see the chart?" She glanced around the room.

3.6   WHAT IS THE *PEACE PROCESS*?

"Now, let's form a phrase by taking one word from each column. Who would like to share their phrase?" Christine asked.

"Love to meditate," Janet spoke up.

"Okay, good. Anyone else?" Christine prompted.

"God wants us to laugh." Dixie contributed.

"Yes, God wants us to laugh," Christine chuckled.

"Still be in the moment," Bonnie suggested.

"That sounds pleasant," Christine observed.

"Unlimited being," Grace shared.

Sonja raised her hand. Christine called on her.

"Gift of joy," Sonja said proudly.

Gary called out, "Love in action."

"Beautiful, thank you." Christine addressed the group. "What inspired phrases you are creating!" She smiled. "Darlene, you're next."

"Trust," Darlene said slowly, searching for a match in the *Process* column. "Divine order," she completed.

"Excellent!" Christine exclaimed as she turned to Sally.

"Steps for harmony," Sally blurted.

"Creative teaching," Dave said.

"Creative teaching. Yeah, I like it. Dave, that's good. This exercise itself is creative teaching! You know, when I was teaching the *Peace Process* on retreat in Costa Rica, I wanted to have all my charts prepared ahead of time. Spirit would have nothing of that—so the paper was blank. At the group meeting, I turned to the flip chart and in that instant knew what to do. Spirit said—*play the word association game for Peace Process.*" Christine smiled.

Joan raised her hand. "God is the source of all creation."

"Lovely," Christine nodded.

"Unlimited creation?" Janet suggested.

"We just keep creating, don't we?" Christine asked.

"Balanced function," Ros piped up.

"Balanced function," Christine echoed.

"So, who else has a phrase to describe the *Peace Process*? Did we miss anybody?"

"I had God function," Dixie added.

"The God function," Christine mused. "The *Peace Process* is the God function. I think we'll end this session on that high note. Everyone has shared something profound. Thank you!"

3.7   EXERCISE

1.   Make a commitment to form a month-long *Peace BEE* habit. Each day you practice, mark your calendar with an "X".

    a.   *Breathe.* Take sixteen breaths to super-charge the blood with oxygen.

    b.   *Energize.* Tilt your head to the right and then to the left to send fresh oxygen to the brain.

    c.   *Embrace.* Wrap your arms around the shoulders and accept yourself with a big hug.

2.   Share *Peace BEE* with your family, friends, neighbors, co-workers, and community. Name the people you might teach.

3.   List your own *Peace Process* word association phrases.

4

Peace Process Worksheet

All good, virtue, happiness and
peace of mind results from love.
Love is the root of all virtues
and the sacrificing struggle for
realization of unity.

—Babaji Nagaraj

"Welcome back from the break." Christine spoke into the hand-held microphone to the group of Unity chaplains. "Please take a Peace Process Worksheet, and pass the rest around the room. We'll go through the six steps of the *Peace Process* together when everyone has a copy." Christine smiled at Gary as she handed him the worksheets.

"Now, the *Peace Process* is built on a Six-Discipline Model of the mind. Before we learn how to think a thought of peace, we will *Discover* what is on our mind that is not peaceful. You know, the brain is a problem-solver and it wants to do its job. And, if there are no problems, the brain wants to be useful and it will create them.

41

According to Edgar Cayce, the father of holistic health, the mind never sleeps. So, the brain is very creative and we struggle when we don't channel our energy appropriately."

Darlene raised her hand. "Darlene?" Christine called on her.

"Someone once asked me what would happen if we didn't have hope. And, I thought how important hope is to me—and how it's a rung on the ladder back to the Christ self. So, hope becomes faith, and then faith becomes trust—which puts me back in touch with my divine nature," Darlene shared.

"Right." Christine nodded. "Trust is faith in the Lord under conditions of uncertainty and it's the foundation of any relationship. We must trust that God brings what is the highest good for all. Without faith and trust, we try to control everything because we have no relationship with God. So, hope is where we begin finding our faith."

"When I don't remember to have faith, there is always hope," Darlene confirmed.

"Yes, Darlene, at that point, you are separated from your divine nature—but, you still have hope. A lot of people without faith feel as though they walk alone, and that is what takes their peace," Christine observed.

4.1   DISCOVER THE PROBLEM

"And so, we begin the *Peace Process* with a question. What takes your peace?" Christine asked.

The chaplains picked up their pens and began to write.

"Think of something that is taking your peace away—or has taken your peace from you, or maybe will take your peace. It doesn't matter how trivial it seems, because if it takes your peace, it is significant. Any upset you have, no matter how small, is a trigger for something that's going on at a deeper level within you. We want to take a look at what that might be so you can move that energy out the door," Christine explained.

"The real point in this first step is to *Discover* the root cause, because if you don't, you will create a similar situation. Sure, it will take a different form. It won't be that person. It will be this person. It won't be that thing. It will be this thing. But, the energy will be the same. For example, you might blame potato chips when you step on the scale. Well, it's not the potato chips taking your peace! The root cause may be some emotional insecurity that reaches outside to satisfy the emptiness within."

Several people were still writing, so Christine continued with a story of her own.

"There are all kinds of reasons to come to the *Peace Process.* I suffered a personal bankruptcy at a time when I was making a million dollars writing medical software. Now you might say, how did you manage that one?" Christine laughed. "Well, my first husband and I owned a miniature golf course named Tiki Tee on Route 192 by the Melbourne Mall. One day, the newspaper headline read: 'STAY INDOORS.' It was because of the encephalitis mosquito."

"Wow!" Ros looked up.

"So, there went our million-dollar golf course. And, I learned a really valuable lesson from the bankruptcy—I am not my money."

"Hmm." Janet put her pen down.

"That experience enabled me to share what happens after you go through bankruptcy. You are still a child of God!"

4.2   ENVISION THE SOLUTION

"Has everyone uncovered something they feel is taking their peace?" Christine glanced around the room. "Now that you have identified what takes your peace, the second step is to *Envision* a solution. We're not really trying to solve problems in the *Peace Process*—we dis-solve problems by changing our perceptions and applying love. The higher energy of love transcends problems created at lower vibrations. The *Peace Process* is one thought that runs on a simple model of the mind like a program on a computer. The *Peace Process* combines the head, which is the hardware, and the heart, which is the software, into one fully-functioning system as it was designed by God."

In the front row, Gary nodded.

"*Envision* uses the faculty of imagination. Just imagine how you would like to see your situation change. In other words, how could you make it better? I'm sure that God supports you working things out for the highest good of all. *Envision* what you desire, what you wish for, and then use your imagination to see it, feel it, taste it, touch it. Put some real energy into your imagined outcome. From the field of all possibilities, this is your opportunity for improvement. Now, write down how you imagine your ideal situation."

As the chaplains picked up their pens, Christine began another story.

"For me, what takes my peace is when my bank balance is low. Last month, I wrote a check to my husband's ex-wife, which left $1.45 in my account. I was upset with June for not including me in the budgeting for Tom's birthday party. Now, if you understand projection, you know that my problem is not really about her. But, I perceive she is taking the money, which means I don't have enough—she triggers my lack of abundance. So, I wrote on my worksheet that I'm irritated when June asks for money. It is important to be honest and tell the truth of how you feel."

Christine paused. "Well, how could I see this differently? What could I do that would be nice? I thought to invite her to dinner and cook for her, because I am sorry that I project my issue onto her. So, I write on my worksheet to call June and invite her for dinner."

Christine continued, "Later, I suggested that we have the whole family for Thanksgiving. So, I cooked a twenty-eight pound turkey and we fed ten people. I felt good about sharing Thanksgiving and we had a lot of fun. Discovering what took my peace, and imagining how I could do something nice shifted the energy."

Gary looked up and put his pen down.

"And, if you don't decide to shift, then you stay stuck in your stuff. The risk is you forget your divine self and you miss out on being the love that you are. We can find the motivation for moving through our issues by first believing our situation can be different. Then we can reframe our thoughts and motivate ourselves to change our thinking," Christine recommended.

A few of the others finished writing.

"See, for the last sixteen years the children typically had Thanksgiving dinner with their mother. Once I decided to prepare a nice meal for everyone, the universe took care of the rest. As a gift, June brought me beautiful kitchen towels with sunflowers on them. Through forgiveness we remember our Christ self, and our life becomes a joyful song."

Darlene smiled approvingly at Christine.

"There's no need to stay stuck in our story. It's just a story and we can change the ending. Move grievances out the door and energy will move in a positive direction," Christine concluded.

4.3   PLAN FOR PEACE

"So, what are the activities that will make our dreams come true? Let's be practical dreamers and develop a *Plan* of action for peace. The *Plan* identifies what you are going to do and schedules when you will do it. Your commitment to follow the *Plan* is what separates the dreamers from the doers. Now, write down one or two things that you could do to realize your vision and goal of peace," Christine encouraged.

Once more, the chaplains picked up their pens.

"I'll give you a simple example. Let's say you *Discover* a need to be more grateful and *Envision* writing a gratitude journal. Your *Plan* might include putting pen to paper and considering your positive feelings. The action you will take is to write a page every morning. And, before you go to bed at night, make a commitment to fill another page. You might be grateful that the sun comes up. You can write about anything! One year, I went through a depression and I needed to find something to be grateful for. So, I decided that if I flossed my teeth every day, that meant I could be thankful for caring, and that made each day a success. So, to move your energy in a positive direction, be grateful."

"Mm-hmm," Sheila looked up thoughtfully.

"Let's take a few more minutes to jot down your ideas." Christine paused while the chaplains wrote.

"Now, does everyone feel like they have a good *Plan*?"

A few of the chaplains nodded.

"Okay, let's *Work* the *Plan* by sending love to what's taking our peace. With heartfelt blessing, you will feel uplifted, and your problems will dis-solve. Lower energy waits to be loved. The *Peace Process* is a spiritual process, which means the *Work* happens through the power of loving thoughts. So, is everyone ready to connect with love?" Christine asked.

4.4   WORK FOR HARMONY

"All right then, I will guide you through a meditation. Please put your pens down and place your feet flat on the floor. Close your eyes, and we will center ourselves with three deep breaths. Inhale slowly—then exhale. Let's take two more breaths. Inhale from below your bellybutton and fill your lungs. As you exhale, let me hear you say *ahh*. One more time, inhale and fill from your toes, lift your shoulders up—and when you're ready to exhale, say *ahh . . .*"

"*Ahh . . .*"

"Now, we offer up our conflict, our little piece of Armageddon—the great battle between good and evil. You know, you can create a new thought by simply rearranging the letters in the words GOOD and EVIL. With the letter 'I' we take responsibility for our actions. 'LOVE' is our only function. And, the three remaining letters spell 'GOD.' The new paradigm is I LOVE GOD," Christine shared.

"Now, hold lightly in your heart the issue that takes your peace. Feel the pain it has caused you and the grief you still feel. Wrap the sorrow, doubt, and fear in your arms. Say to yourself, 'I am sorry, I love you, please forgive me.' Holy Spirit reminds us to bless and not to criticize, condemn, or complain. When you notice a behavior you don't like, bless it anyway—and feel your heart expand with joy."

Christine continued. "Thank you, God, that we are able to express love as we share with one another. Thank you, Jesus, for your demonstration of forgiveness on the cross. We honor you in the *Peace Process* by sending love—in every situation. And, we thank the angels for uplifting us as we release our conflict so that by beginning with ourselves we might contribute to world peace."

4.5   MEASURE THE LOVE

"When you're ready, you can open your eyes." Christine paused. "During the meditation, you allowed your mind to wander—where did your thoughts go? Were you thinking about what you have to do tomorrow? If Spirit spoke to you, jot down what you remember. Take a few minutes and write down what happened on your inward journey."

When Joan put her pen down, Christine began again. "Next, we will *Measure* the quality of the love you sent. Evaluate your love on a scale from zero to ten. If you felt nothing in your heart, give yourself a zero. If you really felt like—wow, that's the end of that issue—give yourself a ten and we'll celebrate with you!" Christine smiled. "All right. Who wants to share their score with the group?"

"Eleven!" Fran exclaimed from the front row.

"Well, you just freed yourself. The universe will take care of whatever was bothering you," Christine assured Fran. "Your blessing is a form of energy that has persistence, with a life of its own. The energy you've sent out will multiply and be given back to you. So, expect good things!"

Ros raised her hand.

"I had about a five. I'm not ready to release my issue," she observed.

"Well, congratulations on your awareness, Ros. Although a five is lukewarm, and energy with that temperature won't dis-solve your problem. So, what can we do when we're not ready to release our issues?" Christine asked the group. "We feedback our insights to create a new *Plan* that we are willing to execute. And then, we make another attempt to send love."

"Carol?" Christine acknowledged.

"Zero," Carol said.

"Nothing happened?" Christine asked.

"This situation is out of my hands. The best way I know to deal with it is not to deal with it at all—for my own peace of mind," Carol explained.

"So, you're not willing to send positive energy?" Christine inquired.

"No." Carol shook her head.

"We don't have control over every situation, but we do have freewill and a heart. God does not step in and tell us what to do because we don't have to do anything!" Christine exclaimed. "God's gift to us is the gift of life. With each breath we have a new opportunity to bless."

"I do believe that," Carol agreed. "But, I feel that I need to protect my heart by isolating this one issue—and that enables me to deal with other ones. It's all about protection."

"Carol, the best protection we can have is a loving heart that extends forgiveness. There are no walls to protect us because, in truth, there is no separation between us. We are one."

Christine spoke to the group. "That reminds me of a time when my own score was zero. Another woman was taking my peace, and I thought I had no control over the situation. My friend and I would get together and talk about this woman. Finally, I told my friend I'm not going to bad-mouth her anymore. When she comes to mind, I'm just going to bless her. Anyway, nothing else was working!"

Carol nodded sympathetically.

"Well, now my friend and I had nothing to talk about anymore, so our friendship fell apart. It was clear that this friendship was based on negative energy. And, as I blessed this other woman, I became aware of how often she came to mind. The negative energy wanted to be fed, but I had made the choice to bless instead. I began to bless her family—her kids and her husband. It was difficult because I was jealous of the close working relationship she had with my husband, but I blessed her anyway. Then, I realized her behavior was the same as my own a decade before. You see, the energy that I had put out multiplied and came back to me. So, I turned my marriage over to God. And, I learned that you can bless anything."

Dixie raised her hand.

"Okay, what have you got, Dixie?"

"An eight," Dixie shared.

"So, you're feeling pretty good?"

"I'm working on it," Dixie said.

"That's great, keep sending the love. Give yourself more love. And when you do, you feed your own soul."

Ruby spoke up. "Christine, I only gave myself a five."

"Why is that, Ruby?" Christine asked.

"Because I was thinking on a much larger scale. I wasn't thinking of a co-worker or friend or family or neighbor. I was thinking of world peace."

"So, what's the problem—you can't send love to world peace? You know, we all want it."

"There's not too much we can do about it," Ruby said.

"That's not true!" Christine exclaimed. "Your fear is that we don't have world peace now."

"Yes," Ruby confirmed.

"But, as long as you believe that, the world shows up that way for you. If you can give up your belief that there is no world peace, then you can light the world. Each one of us is an important part of the immune system in the larger body and each one has a job to do." Christine glanced around the room. "You're all heart cells, and that means your job is to love," Christine declared.

"Hmm!" Ruby was thoughtful. "Well, I envisioned loving one and all and having world peace."

"That's good, but at the same time, ask how you can bring peace to yourself. You can be a catalyst for change. Remember, it was John F. Kennedy who said we will send a man to the moon and return him safely to Earth. Did he personally send a man to the moon? No. Did he personally bring the man back safely? No. It was his vision that inspired everyone else. And, going to the moon gave humanity a new perspective as we looked upon the beauty of our planet. So, we each need to do our part—and never lose hope!"

Christine turned to Janet.

"Well, I put down a seven and then I had to pull it back to about a six or five, because I don't think I have clarity about what the real problem is," Janet shared.

"Okay, I would be happy to work with you on that, and again I'm not trying to fix you, but I can mirror you. I can hold the sacred space and listen so you can express yourself. Let's talk later," Christine offered.

"Thanks," Janet said.

"Darlene?"

"I'm not sure. I guess my score was about a five, and it's because I'm not willing to let go yet. There must be a reason I'm holding on," Darlene observed.

"Sure!" Christine nodded. "You choose to be right rather than happy."

The chaplains laughed.

"One other thing," Darlene continued. "I used to ship all my problem people to an island and that's how I got rid of them."

"Did they have to stay there?" Christine grinned.

"Yes, for awhile. I didn't realize then that I was the prisoner," Darlene said. "And, at some point I had to get all those people back. I don't know how many people were on the island, but

Reverend Charles and I went over there and put them on a big boat. I'll tell you the truth—I didn't remember who they were when they got off the island—I only remember the smiles on their faces," Darlene explained. "In reality, those smiles were mine, because I was finally free. So, I realize that my chaplain work and everything I'm involved in puts me in a place where I don't need to ship people off to islands anymore. I can love them just like you're saying. But, in this particular situation, I'm not ready yet."

"Does that mean the island is available for use?" Ros asked.

Everyone laughed heartily.

"Let's give Darlene some energy to boost her five, and for her honesty." Christine began to clap and the others joined in.

"*Measure* is about rating the quality of the love we send. After all, you deserve to know that you are loving. You are forgiven when you forgive, so bless all those who have helped to move you along your spiritual path," Christine smiled.

4.6   VALUE THE PROGRESS

"Okay, the last step is to *Value* the progress you've made in our time together. Let's take a few minutes now and write about what you've learned. Reinforce this positive experience with your gratitude. Be thankful for yourself and each other. Thank yourself for taking the time to go through your stuff. Be thankful for the stories we shared, because they help us remember. Now, does anyone care to share what they're grateful for and what they *Value* from the *Peace Process*?"

A hand went up. "Sheila?" Christine called on her.

"I am grateful I did the process, because it brought me clarity," Sheila offered.

"That's great. Clarity is awesome—what a gift!" Christine exclaimed.

In the back of the room, Darlene raised her hand. "Darlene," Christine called.

"I am grateful that I was able to share that I didn't quite make it to a ten," Darlene confessed.

"You know, I think you did make it." Christine smiled. "You gained awareness and you were honest. So, you get points for that."

Christine looked to the person in front of her. "Want to share?"

"Me?" Barbara asked.

"Yes," Christine nodded.

Barbara read from her worksheet. "I am grateful and thankful that again I see the truth that love and forgiveness of myself and others is the true path to spiritual happiness."

"Yea!" Darlene exclaimed.

Barbara continued, "I am thankful for my teachers and Christine."

"Gee, thank you, thank you." Christine smiled. "Let's give Barbara a round of applause!"

The chaplains clapped.

"And, thanks to everyone. The *Peace Process* is a spiritual process. You know, Jesus taught us about love and forgiveness. We're finding different ways to apply his teaching," Christine concluded. "Now it's time to form our circle."

When all hands were joined, Darlene began the closing prayer.

4.7 EXERCISE

1. Use the Peace Process Worksheet found in Appendix D and complete the six steps on your journey to inner peace.

2. Did you *Discover* something that takes your peace? Might there be a deeper issue waiting to be uncovered?

3. Can you decide to take responsibility for your issue and choose to bless instead of blame?

5

The Blessed Hope

Aho Sacred Tree of Life,
The root of every tree,
Thank you for giving
The gifts you give to me.

Aho Willow, tree of love,
Teach me to bend,
Til I come full circle,
Each relation as my friend.

—Jamie Sams

"You live in paradise!" The attractive African American woman exclaimed as Christine opened the large glass door to her home.

"I know," Christine confessed cheerfully. "Hi, Wanda."

"Hi, Dr. Christine." Wanda was right on time for her scheduled appointment.

"How are you?" Christine gave her friend a heart hug.

"I'm fine and I am really excited about our session today." Wanda followed Christine into her comfortable den and sat down on the ivory leather sofa with a green pillow behind her back.

Christine settled on the couch facing her friend. "I saw you on the front cover of *Space Coast Woman*. There you were! *Dr. Wanda Bethea Making a Difference in People's Lives*."

"Oh, it's a life-size picture, isn't it? Very striking. I was so surprised to see myself in print." Wanda seemed pleased with the feature publication.

"You had an enormous smile," Christine remembered. "You looked positively radiant!"

"Yes, I felt good that day," Wanda reflected.

"I enjoyed the article," Christine told her.

"Thank you, thank you—the reporter did a great job. She captured a lot . . ." Wanda paused.

". . . of who you are," Christine finished her sentence. It had been a surprise to read that Wanda earned Master's degrees in Teaching, Psychology, and Counseling before completing her Doctorate at Columbia University in New York.

"I loved what she said about making a difference. I like to believe I do that. It's part of my job and my mission." Wanda's face lit up as she spoke.

"Mmm, I can tell we're on the same path." Christine smiled gently. She had been entrusted with an important mission and felt eager to make a difference, too.

"We are, Dr. Christine, we certainly are," Wanda confirmed with a nod and a big grin.

"Well, I have something significant to share with you today, and that is the *Peace Process*," Christine said with anticipation.

"Yes, tell me more about the *Peace Process*." Wanda leaned forward.

5.1 SIX-DISCIPLINE MODEL

Christine sat back on the couch and began to tell her story. "It was the most embarrassing moment of my professional career. I was with Tom in London teaching my *Software Risk Management* seminar. One of the students asked me, 'How does risk fit in the big picture?' I turned to write something on the board, but my mind went blank. After class, I went back to the hotel room and Tom asked 'How did it go today, honey?' And, I said 'Not so good. The students asked me a question that I couldn't answer.' I remember Tom saying, 'Don't worry, we'll work on it together when we get home.' The question of how does risk fit in the big picture would become my Zen koan!"

"What exactly is a koan?" Wanda wondered.

"Well, a koan is an enigma that confounds the individual mind, which only knows by the difference. A koan is a riddle in the form of a paradox that brings intuitive knowledge from a universal mind through your own desire, meditation, and observation."

"I see," Wanda nodded.

"In March of 1996, Tom and I developed a model of the mind that we named the Six-Discipline Model (see Appendix A). The Six-Discipline Model is a simple process diagram of the human brain that can run any thought. The model is validated by the scientific method (see Appendix B), a proven philosophy of inquiry first described by René Descartes."

"Ah." Wanda blinked.

"On January 17, 1997, I drew the Six-Discipline Model with help from a higher intelligence that gave me direction to simplify my process diagram. Tom and I wrote a paper and presented our model at the International Council on Systems Engineering Symposium in Los Angeles. The following year, my text *Managing Risk* was published describing the model as *the grail within each one of us.* But, I began to wonder *what makes the grail holy?*"

5.2   AN INSPIRATION FOR PEACE

"In March of 1998, I attended a spiritual conference in Miami where it was my privilege to meet authors like Neale Donald Walsch, James Redfield, and Wayne Dyer. That event was such an emotional experience for me. When I returned home, I was inspired to write the thought of world peace on the Six-Discipline Model, and that became the *Peace Process* (see Appendix C)."

"Oh, really?" Wanda listened carefully.

"At mid-life, I'd been through a divorce, a bankruptcy, and then the death of my mother. Dr. Dyer's audio program

Transformations: You'll See It When You Believe It really helped me through those tough times. I found his message so beneficial that I listened over and over to pull myself out of depression."

Wanda nodded sympathetically.

Christine continued softly, "In 1999, my second husband denied winking at his co-worker, and I was devastated again. As a result, I had to fix my own self-esteem. So, I decided to send myself to the Yoga College of India in Beverly Hills for nine weeks."

"Hmm." Wanda raised her eyebrows.

"I began to play piano and walk the beach. In the year 2000, I bought the book *A Course in Miracles* and joined a study group. Every day I would look forward to the lesson in the workbook."

"Ahh . . ." Wanda approved.

5.3   LITTLE YELLOW STICKIES

"The following month, I went to Boston for my youngest sister's bridal shower, and I left love notes on little yellow stickies all over the house. When I spoke with Tom that evening, he didn't mention the love notes. Finally, I asked 'How did you like the little yellow stickies?' And he said, 'What yellow stickies?' Well, I had left them everywhere—they would have been hard to miss. That's when I realized my stepson must have taken the little yellow stickies! Tom spoke with him, and he denied seeing the notes. It was a dilemma for me, because I knew I had left the notes, but Tom didn't find them. And, I didn't want to accuse Ryan, who was only fifteen years old."

"I understand," Wanda said.

"After I hung up the phone, I cried out to God. With my hands raised up, I demanded he take me now because I did not want to be in this place where there was not enough love to go around. I wanted to go home, back to God—and, I meant it with all my heart."

Wanda listened intently.

"Later, Tom told me that Ryan apologized to him for removing the love notes. The next time I went out of town, I left little yellow stickies for both boys. I found the love that I was looking for—it comes from an unending source within myself!"

"Mmm . . ." Wanda smiled.

5.4   THE WINGS OF PEACE

"I was raised Catholic, and when I was thirteen, I chose Christine as my confirmation name. My intention was to become the feminine Christ. But, for many years, until I was forty-three, Christine slept in my subconscious."

Wanda nodded.

"It was during the summer of the millennium that I experienced a vision of the peace symbol, and the next day Christine returned to my conscious mind. I saw the sunrise and a dolphin swimming in the ocean, practiced yoga on the beach, and wrote in my journal: *The wings of peace are the past and future, which we have created. The Holy Grail is the peace of Christ. This morning I understood that yesterday was given me to fulfill my destiny as Christine, prophet of the mental age,*" Christine recalled.

"Oh!" Wanda exclaimed.

"I was teaching yoga at *Yoga with Helena* over on Highland Avenue, and this man named John introduced himself after one of my classes."

"Hmm."

"He told me that he spent thirty years sailing around the world on a boat he built. He grew up in Eau Gallie and came home because his mother was sick. John told me that if I had met him the week before, I probably would have avoided him." Christine paused.

"Now, why is that?" Wanda wondered.

"He said his hair was down to his waist! Anyway, I picked up a strange vibe from him, so I asked for his phone number . . ."

Wanda's eyes widened.

". . . and I invited him for dinner to see if maybe Tom would know who he was."

"Did he?" Wanda asked.

"No, but we had a nice conversation at dinner—both Tom and John are sailors. And, I asked my guidance why this man was so familiar. That's when I noticed an article on my coffee table about Baptiste. He's a yoga teacher in Boston. I couldn't get the name out of my head—Baptiste, Baptiste."

"You had the thought that your new friend might have been John the Baptist?" Wanda guessed.

"I asked him about that. I wondered if he had issues with his neck. You know, Wanda, John the Baptist had his head cut off."

"And . . ."

"He admitted that he did. Then he asked if he could be my disciple!" Christine exclaimed.

"What did you say?" Wanda leaned forward.

"I said no, this time we go together." Christine took a deep breath.

"On October 30, 2000, John came over to my home. I read from *A Course in Miracles*, Lesson 185: *I want the peace of God.* Together we renounced our illusions, joined our minds in truth, and really meant it."

"That's beautiful," Wanda nodded.

"The *Course* says the mind that wants peace must join with other minds, for that is how peace is obtained. And, no one loses and everyone gains when any gift of God has been requested and received." Christine drank from her glass of water.

5.5   I WORK FOR GOD

"Would you like some more?" Wanda picked up the pitcher to refill her own glass.

"Yes, please." Christine rearranged the pillow behind her.

"In December, I considered writing another book. But, then, I decided I'd work for God instead. A week later, I went on an all-expenses paid week at a ski resort in Aspen, Colorado."

66

"Are you kidding?" Wanda was incredulous.

"No, my neighbor Mary came over and said her sister had a timeshare our family could use, which included a ski package. Tom gave me his frequent flyer miles because he was too busy at work to join me and the children were in school—so, I went alone."

"How lucky for you!" Wanda grinned.

"During the day, I skied Snowmass with my ski instructor, Christopher. And, at night, I took notes—it was like going to school. I don't watch television at home—we don't have cable—but, one night I turned on the TV and Oprah was on."

"I think she's great," Wanda confided.

"God was showing me that I would be on Oprah's show." Christine smiled. "Maybe we can both be on Oprah!"

"Wouldn't that be fun?" Wanda laughed.

"So, in the spring, I was guided to open *Yoga with Christine* and . . ."

". . . that's when we met—I came to take your yoga class," Wanda interrupted.

"That's right, Wanda." Christine continued, "Only three months after the yoga studio opened, I was led to go on an 18-day pilgrimage to India. The timing didn't seem right, but I had a dream that I was sitting in a train station, regretting that I missed the train. Because I trusted the emotion surrounding that dream, I made a commitment to take the trip. And then—Bret, Brenda, Gretchen, and Jill showed up to teach my classes."

"Where God guides, he provides," Wanda chuckled.

5.6   CREATING MY HEART'S DESIRE

"I'm not sure if you know this, but when I returned home from the pilgrimage in India, that plane was one of the first to land in New York City after the Twin Towers tragedy."

"Oh, my!"

"I was determined to be the change I wanted to see in the world. At the yoga studio, Linda Sands began an eleven-week series of DreamQuest classes on *How to Create Your Heart's Desire*. Wanda, do you know Linda?"

"No, I don't." Wanda shook her head.

"She helps students identify personal, business, and social dreams and goals. My personal dream is to reflect the peace of God and bring peace to every mind. In the second week of class, I recognized that my fear of people's judgment has been an obstacle for me. On the other hand, I wrote in my DreamQuest workbook: *I please God when I am true to my higher self.*"

"Someone once said, 'The people who mind don't matter and the people who matter don't mind.' Now, who was that?" Wanda asked.

"I think it was Dr. Seuss!" Christine laughed. "Well, I managed to get beyond my own critical voice. By week three of the DreamQuest series, I drew a heart to symbolize my love for God. I made a smiley face to show joy, and I promised to write about my relationship with God and to share the good news with others," Christine explained.

"Ah, your life's work." Wanda nodded.

"In week six, I affirmed that *I, Christine, truly deserve in every cell of my being, to have, share, and be the love of God.* I'll never forget the night of the seventh class on commitment, when I showed up in a bridal gown. Linda was delighted that I said 'I do' to my personal dream. The vow I made to my creative life force was: *I, Christine, now commit myself totally—mind, body, and soul—to my DreamQuest of bringing peace to every mind.*"

"I've seen a photo of you in the bridal dress," Wanda remembered.

"Well, I bought the dress from Goodwill, because I never actually had a wedding gown of my own. Tom and I left work early one day and were married by a Justice of the Peace. When I married my first husband, I borrowed his sister's wedding dress."

Wanda picked up her glass of water and sipped.

Christine continued, "When I posed in the gown as the bride of Christ, my bouquet was several of my grandmother's gorgeous purple cattleyas. I always wanted to be like my grandmother. She raised beautiful orchids, and it was a blessing for me when I inherited some of her plants. After all these years, her orchids still bloom with a heavenly fragrance!"

"How sweet." Wanda put her glass down on the coaster.

5.7 OUR LOVE STORY

"Glenda Green painted my angel portrait with one of those orchids in her hair. When the painting arrived on June 30, 2003, I ordered the angel's natal chart using the time of her delivery by United Parcel Service!"

"I don't understand the connection between the chart and UPS," Wanda said.

"Every idea is born in a place and time. My angel's delivery at 4:07 PM by UPS created the basis for her astrological profile. Together, we form a water cycle—I am a Pisces sun sign with Cancer rising, and she is Cancer with Scorpio rising."

"Oh, I get it. I understand." Wanda nodded.

"Then on November 4, 2003, I gave a presentation at Holy Name of Jesus—my father's church in Indialantic—and he unveiled my angel painting. On that same day, the most powerful solar flare ever recorded erupted!" Christine exclaimed.

"Hmm. That would generate lots of magnetic energy," Wanda considered.

"Yes, with the spirit of love my mind expanded into a global awareness whose acronym is KI-LIME: Knowledge, Intuition, Logic, Imagination, Memory, and Emotion (see Appendix E). I call the model of this universal mind Peace Consciousness (see Appendix F). The missing piece of the Six-Discipline Model had been found, which resolved my koan. You see, Wanda, in the big picture . . . *there is no risk!*"

"Marvelous," Wanda smiled.

"The new Peace Consciousness shows the dissolution of ego, and is validated by the Harmonic Concordance (see Appendix G). Wanda, are you familiar with the Harmonic Concordance?" Christine asked.

Wanda shook her head. "No, tell me about it."

"Well, John Mirehiel used a software program to discover a unique planetary alignment that would occur on November 8, 2003. Two grand trines in water and earth signs formed a Star of David in the sky, and John named it the Harmonic Concordance."

"The shift of ages!" Wanda exclaimed.

"The morning of the Harmonic Concordance, I gave a keynote speech, *Rapture: Our Love Story*. I told the ancient love story between Creator and creation, between heart and soul, between divinity and humanity. Next to me on an easel was my lovely angel. I shared the three keys to a divine relationship: commitment, communication, and trust."

Wanda was thoughtful. "Ah, commitment, communication, and trust."

"As a bride in a new marriage with Christ, how would I feel? I would have made a vow to love, honor, and cherish. I would freely share the love that I am and trust in love's return." Christine smiled.

"You know, it's just like the little yellow stickies. There is plenty of love to go around," Wanda mused.

"Yes, that's the universal dialogue of love! You know, the name of each discipline in Peace Consciousness can be transliterated to form the elements of a musical ratio E/G. These harmonic vibrations combine as language, silently speaking messages (see Appendix H) and drawing symbols (see Appendix I). Our love story is about that eternal communication between lover and beloved!" Christine beamed.

5.8   PEACE OF MIND

"When Tom and I moved to Merritt Island in 2004, I closed *Yoga with Christine* and officially changed my name to Elaine Marie Christine. My angel taught me to send love to what takes my peace. Now I want to teach the *Peace Process* to health care professionals, like you, Wanda." Christine's hand reached out to touch Wanda's. "The ultimate goal and my personal mission is to incorporate this method to help bring *peace to every mind*."

"That's brilliant." Wanda's soft brown eyes sparkled behind the frame of her glasses.

"I think of the *Peace Process* as the blessed hope that remains in Pandora's box when all the evil of the world has flown." Christine's hands were animated.

"Oh, what a wonderful metaphor!" Wanda exclaimed.

"So, shall we begin the *Peace Process* and see how it might help you to help other people?" Christine asked.

"I would love to learn about the *Peace Process*. I can show my clients how it works—and use it for myself as well!" Wanda was enthusiastic.

"It's a wonderful self-help tool once you learn it. Chaplains can use it in their ministry and counselors can apply it in their practice. I have used it successfully within groups of people either on individual issues or one that concerns the whole. For example, a family could use it," Christine explained.

"Does it take a particular amount of time to do this process?" Wanda wanted to know.

"The smallest amount of time that I've used with a group was 20 minutes—I presented it for the local Rotary Club."

"So, do you think a therapist could use it in a family session?" Wanda asked.

"Absolutely," Christine agreed.

"My goodness, that would be so valuable in my work, I know—and in the practice of any therapist, counselor, or psychologist for that matter. Yes, in clinical work, that would be a great asset," Wanda nodded. "I guess a teacher could use it for the class!" Wanda's excitement grew as she considered the possibilities.

"Now you see why I'm so inspired to share this!" Christine laughed heartily.

"Are you saying you would use this for any particular student—or for any class of students?" Wanda wondered.

"Even a whole class of students." Christine liked the dynamic of group sessions. "For any group working together, the method brings a common base that allows people to air their issues. As you will see, Wanda, the *Peace Process* begins with a problem.

We don't let folks stay in the problem; we move them into solution. The time spent is about a 20/80 ratio of problem to solution."

Wanda nodded.

"Let's say you only have ten minutes. You would spend two minutes on the problem and eight minutes on the solution."

Wanda understood the benefit of structuring the available time. "Ah, so you don't get stuck. The whole idea is to move forward, that's why it's a process. I see—you get out of the problem."

"Yes, that's it! The solution is to dis-solve a problem by sending love to what's taking our peace."

"That's exciting—when do we start?" Wanda was eager to begin.

"Let's start right now!" Christine jumped up from the couch. She took a moment to turn the video recorder on and adjust it to capture their one-hour *Peace Process* session for future use.

5.9   EXERCISE

1.   Every person is blessed with natural talents. List your God-given gifts.

2.   Life presents challenges. Identify the adversity in your life and describe what those hardships taught you.

3.   How does what you have learned help you to make a difference in your world?

PART III

Compassion and Peace

Life is energy, pure creative energy.
Our creative dreams and yearnings
come from a divine source.
As we move toward our dreams,
we move toward our divinity.

—Julia Cameron

Part III describes five individual *Peace Process* sessions that I facilitated during the years 2005–2006. Sessions were videotaped, transcribed, and edited. Although it seems that friends are coming to me for help, I realize that each one brings an important message to guide my own spiritual journey.

Chapter 6, The Spiritual Entrepreneur. Wanda Bethea is a psychologist with a private counseling practice and a big heart, who needs help quantifying the value of her service. Together, we imagine an article describing a success story for Wanda. She has the vision and the passion—but is her faith strong enough to make her dreams come true?

Chapter 7, Envision Peace. Deeply in debt, Barbara Hodal has the weight of worry on her shoulders. Barbara is working to overcome barriers of discouragement and frustration, and planning to teach perseverance as a key spiritual practice on her own journey to peace of mind. She claims to be God's Healer, but will Barbara remain true to her purpose in the face of obstacles?

Chapter 8, Plan for Inner Peace. Louis Gross arrives at AquaTerra for help with some of his challenges. I ask Lou to talk about what makes him happy, and he reveals that he is a teacher with healing hands and a soothing voice. Lou's ultimate challenge is to calm the critical voice inside his head, giving himself the empathy and compassion that he wants to share.

Chapter 9, A Habit of Love. Audrice Collins digs deep to uncover old negative thought patterns of jealousy and abandonment. Will she be able to heal these unresolved childhood issues by sending love to her deceased parents? Audrice blesses the old dramas to release her negative emotions.

Chapter 10, My Peaceful Purpose. Kim Fisichella learns the *Peace Process* at the White Eagle Retreat Center in Costa Rica. Kim's purpose is to be a healer—but first she must balance the stress in her own life. Kim plans for harmony at home by setting boundaries that honor each of her relationships, and being strong in her spiritual ideals.

6

The Spiritual Entrepreneur

Peace be to you, fear not.

—Genesis [43:23]

"Wanda, the first step in the *Peace Process* is the *Discover* discipline," Christine said as she handed her a sign with 2-inch gold letters. "The color for *Discover* is red like our blood, which represents passion. The warm life-force energy of *Discover* is the root where we begin."

Christine continued, "Let's talk about some injustice that you feel—a deep issue that keeps you from peace. It may be about another person, a place, a thing—it doesn't matter what it is. As we discuss that issue, we will learn about the *Peace Process*. Choose something that you are passionate about." Christine paused to give Wanda time to consider her feelings.

6.1   IDENTIFY THE ISSUE

"Oh yes, I can think of something right away. For me, what I feel deeply about has to do with being in business and making money. I want to be kind to people and do what's in the best interest of my clients, but I also need to earn a living for myself and my family."

"So, you want a benevolent business that combines those two worlds," Christine rephrased Wanda's thought.

"Yes! I don't want to be so competitive, so sharkish that I can't bring something that is really positive to another person."

"Are you saying that you need to learn how to place a value on your helpfulness?" Christine asked.

"Yeah, the helpfulness of what I can give—what I can provide," Wanda clarified.

"Right, the value of giving without feeling guilty about getting something in return," Christine pressed on.

"Yes, I am in business for that, but I am also in business, I believe, to provide something that's almost transcendent—that's what I'm talking about." Wanda zeroed in on her target issue.

"You are not only focused on the person, you are focused on their higher self," Christine reiterated.

"Higher being. Exactly."

"You want to help that person get to their next happy state." Christine reframed the issue.

"Exactly, and I want them to know that, yes, there is a price for that," Wanda nodded.

"You want them to know that you are offering something of real value." Christine stood aside so the video camera captured Wanda's expressions.

"Yes, there is something to be valued. I put a monetary price on my help, yet it's about helping my clients get in touch with a higher self as well."

"Now that's priceless," Christine realized.

"Yes, it is Christine. Yes, it is," Wanda agreed.

"You just want people to recognize that treasure." Christine searched for the root of the issue.

"Yes. Therapists with the same counseling service might not really be coming from the same heart," Wanda observed.

"Wanda, I can tell you have quite a heart. I think we have identified your issue. It is a challenge for you to quantify the value of what you provide. You need help to sort out the contradictions," Christine summarized.

"Yes," Wanda confirmed.

"How can you integrate the self and the selfless so that your spirit soars, sings, and provides value?" Christine asked.

"Exactly, exactly, that's right." Wanda nodded.

6.2   A FIELD OF POSSIBILITY

"Well, within the *Discover* discipline is a field of all possibilities. In our blood, in the DNA, we find a void where there is a potential for the positive and a potential for the negative. The positive possibilities we call opportunity and the negative possibilities we call risk. But in truth, Wanda, you don't know your opportunity until you understand your risk."

"I see, you need to be aware of both the opportunity and the risk."

"Let's think about the pluses and the minuses in your situation. We can't just consider the positive aspects of the higher self—we have to look at the potential negative. What if you didn't provide this kind of counseling service? Would your clients benefit if you were unable to help them because you were forced to get a job that you didn't want to do—just for the money? No, they would suffer."

"You're right." Wanda was thoughtful as she rearranged the pillow behind her.

"In other words, there's a down side. If you don't accept the money, you won't be able to meet your obligations. Money is the value returned." Christine explained the consequence.

"Exactly—and I wouldn't be able to provide my services," Wanda agreed.

"You know inherently within yourself that you must take money, which is an exchange of value. In the barter system, you would do your counseling work and somebody else would give you food, perhaps," Christine considered.

"Yes, that's true!"

"These days, everything is measured monetarily. But mental health is a prerequisite for producing goods and services, so that comes first, and that's what you offer." Christine made her point.

"Okay," Wanda allowed.

"Goods for the body would be something physical like your clothes. But the good for your mind is like the *Peace Process*. We have to place value on both the tangible and the intangible. For you, the counseling is a service for emotional well-being. Look at the negative. If you don't take the money, it means that ultimately you can't continue to offer the service—and the service is needed."

"I do believe that." Wanda knew her practice uplifted the people she saw.

"It's just getting through the old paradigm that says if it's spiritual, then it can't be about money—and it's not. But, it is about value. Let's take the positive path and say that if you do accept the money for compassionate service, there's no contradiction. It's only a false perception. The spiritual way is to provide value, and you will provide value, and value will be returned. It's not that money is bad spiritually. I think that's the misperception here."

"So, that's what we *Discover*!" Wanda exclaimed.

"We *Discover* what is true by knowing what is false."

"Now I see the polarity," Wanda reflected.

"Right, because what is true has always been true. Spiritual service has always had value, but you want your clients to perceive that value as much as you do. Payment in dollars or however they pay is appropriate."

"Okay. In other words, my clients need to *Discover* that, too."

"Clients must pay to perceive value. If they don't pay, they won't," Christine affirmed.

"Exactly, they won't—they won't! That's exactly right. So, this is a discovery process for me—and for them. It reinforces for me what I had hoped people would understand. I help them to *Discover* that I need to be paid and my service is valuable enough to justify that." Wanda began to see that she needed to believe in the value of her own services.

"That's right. Well, I think we have enough inspiration now to move on to the next discipline. There is a lot of passion behind this. Passion is just energy. Part of the energy in a discovery process is a bit of uncertainty mixed with a fear of the unknown. That's what we have to wrestle with. The root of an issue is typically disguised or hidden and it must be dis-covered, un-covered—we have to disrobe it to see what is real."

"Oh, I get it!" Wanda had a moment of clarity.

"Let the fear, guilt, and worry out because that's what is covering the truth. Lift your problem like a dark cloud up to the sun. What does the sun, which is truth, do but shine the cloud away? The cloud cannot exist—the thought will dissipate with the warmth of the sun. The cloud is like a passing thought. So, let go of your guilt. Let that go. We know that money is not bad spiritually. Offer the misperception up, and the sun will shine it away." Christine took the

Discover sign from Wanda and put it down on the coffee table next to the stack of rainbow-colored signs.

"I like that. Offer it up!" As Wanda sipped from her glass of water, she saw her issue from a new perspective.

6.3   CREATE THE VISION

"Now let's go to *Envision*, the second step in the *Peace Process*," Christine said as she gave Wanda the placard labeled *Envision*. "The color for *Envision* is orange, and that is associated with creativity. We're going to create a dream, a goal, and a vision of how you want to be with respect to taking money in your holistic counseling practice. Let's live the dream by writing a new article with the headline: *Dr. Wanda Bethea, Counselor and Healer.*"

"Okay." Wanda was listening carefully.

"I've just provided the headline—now you write the article. What does it say about how you've been successful at showing your clients the value of your counseling? And how you've become so successful that you have expanded—perhaps, providing a wing at the hospital . . ."

"Absolutely." Wanda liked the idea.

"So, accept all the success, like Oprah . . ."

"Ooh." Wanda saw Oprah Winfrey as a kind soul and a role model for many people.

"Have you heard she sponsored a bus that goes around making dreams come true for other people? Think how you can extend yourself by accepting value. As we just discovered, we have to let the blood flow, which is the exchange—no more blood clots!"

"Ahh." Wanda shifted in the chair and tilted her head with a grin on her face.

"And now I want you to paint the vision of your success so that you and Oprah are now peers."

"Hmm. Hmm!" Wanda looked up with surprise.

"Doesn't the sun shine equally on both of you?" Christine questioned.

"Yeah, I guess it does," Wanda realized.

"Describe this article to me. How did you get to be the billionaire that you are, Wanda?" Christine prompted more specifically.

"Well, I have so many people coming to me through word of mouth. They hear about my ability to heal them—to get rid of the demons and to soar emotionally, physically, and spiritually, Dr. Christine. That's what the article says. And people come because I make a difference. They tell their friends and bring their children and their parents to me. I help them to talk about some of the things that are really crippling them—and then they stand tall. It is just marvelous! I am so grateful that they feel healed and say I made a difference."

"Tell me about the book that you wrote. The article says that you wrote a book, and that it was a best seller," Christine intuited.

Wanda threw her head back and laughed, delighted with Christine's impromptu interview. "Oh, yes, I wrote a book and it's all about the different chapters of life—things that happen that make you go *Hmm*. I wrote about raising children, loving your partner, and what I wanted for the world—in government and for the leaders in politics as well as in churches. The book is an allegory, a fairy tale where everybody—Jews, Gentiles, doesn't matter—Arabs, Mexicans, Blacks, Irish, and Italian—where everyone who lives in this world speaks a common language, even though their native languages are different. It's like Star Trek, when Captain Kirk came to the place where all the people communicated through thought. It didn't matter what they looked like or what language they spoke. They just uplifted each other and it became a marvelous world and universe. It's about the coming of a time and a place where we go *Hmm* . . ." Wanda raised her right index finger to her temple, ". . . and understand."

"Well, what is so marvelous is how many languages the book has been translated into," Christine persisted.

"Oh, thank you. It's been quite a journey. It is wonderful that my vision was finally actualized. Thank you for asking about the book." Wanda was pleased to be caught up in the creation of her vision.

"You're welcome. That is a big part of your success. It's just the outreach then to take you from your little community into the world," Christine imagined.

"It's bigger than us, it's bigger. I believe the plan is bigger," Wanda acknowledged.

"I know we will help a lot of people who want in their hearts to help others, but somehow feel a contradiction about accepting money. They don't understand that they can live their passion, that they can really make a difference, because they can let their blood flow and accept that the true value of spirit is priceless."

"Yes. It's almost like tithing, you know?" Wanda raised her eyebrows as she glanced up at Christine. "It occurred to me when you were talking, I never thought about it like that. How do you show the value of the spirit? How is value demonstrated? You tithe." Wanda's intuition was leading her on.

"Let's talk about some of the projects that you've initiated with your millions." Christine invited Wanda to focus on more details of her dream.

"Okay, I have an institute where a lot of people come to be trained and to share where they have been and where they want to go. It's like a university without walls where everyone is a teacher in a mentoring culture. It's an academic, spiritual, and coaching environment. Of course, we provide scholarships to people if they need it. Those who don't need it come joyously and pay. It's a wonderful fellowship at the institute. That is one of my projects."

Christine smiled at Wanda's dynamic imagination.

Wanda continued, "I also have a school for children where you teach them to read and write through music, dance, art, and personal expression. We've got some outstanding teachers there and we pay them very well because they are so inspiring. I want them to feel happy and filled up themselves so they can pass all of that on to the children. I believe every child can learn—you just have to find the right approach, the right learning style. I fill up my teachers so they can fill up the kids."

"And then their cup runs over . . ." Christine knew the benefits would multiply for future generations.

"That's exactly right. Fill up and then share. Those are two of my favorite projects." Wanda was clearly inspired.

"Wonderful! That is a lovely story for those headlines. Live your dreams. It's about painting the picture first and then we live to that dream."

"Beautiful. I was there." Wanda had stepped into her future effortlessly.

"I know, and you will be there again," Christine assured her, reaching for the orange canvas art board.

As she returned the *Envision* sign to Christine, Wanda's face shone with delight. "Thank you, thank you," she said, marveling at the success story she had created.

6.4   THE DREAM IS ALIVE

"Wanda, the discipline *Plan* is the third step in the *Peace Process*," Christine said as she offered her another sign to hold. "The color for *Plan* is a yellow similar to the sun, and it corresponds to personal power and the intellect. Through the *Plan* we assign available resources such as time, talent, and money. People are the greatest resource."

"They are," Wanda agreed.

"And you may have in the beginning, some volunteers. These people are learning from you—perhaps under your teaching. They would then be apprentices that offer assistance. Do you know what I am saying? New volunteers learn from your trained helpers. The volunteers would help achieve the *Plan* to manifest your school, your research center, and the higher learning of the spirit—how to do things with a spiritual heart." Christine had no clue where she got the information that she gave to Wanda.

"Oh, yes. I like that idea." Wanda thought the *Plan* was a meaningful step in the process.

"I know you are very good at planning."

"Yes." Wanda smiled at her highly organized life with mind, body, and spirit intertwined. Wanda's 20-year career as a psychologist, her 34-year marriage to Richard, raising a son, and her enjoyment of four grandchildren proved her management skills. She also found time for yoga and dance.

"So, you can create the schedule and deadlines and then you'll know how much money it costs. That's what you'll need to budget so you'll know how much to charge the people such that you can carry on this very important work." More messages came through Christine.

"You're right." Wanda was glad she did not have to take notes to capture all the good ideas. Christine had mentioned that she would take home a video recording of their session.

THE SPIRITUAL ENTREPRENEUR

"And be published and be able to be translated. Sell the book at a price so that built into that price is not just the cost of the paper and printing but that you also get the translations that are needed to reach out into a world that is bigger than the one we are in now."

"I will remember that. You are exactly right—that is an important part of the *Plan* in order to do the outreach that I *Envision*."

"The outreach is so important because that is your spilling over. This money is not just for you, your bread and water," Christine cautioned.

"No, it's bigger than that," Wanda agreed.

"It's much bigger than that. That's why it's so important and that's why it is important to budget the time to complete the book, however you structure the outline—perhaps give a free lecture on each chapter and record yourself and then transcribe that. It can be something so simple as taping a session that you would have with a friend or a client. Do you know what I'm saying?"

"What an idea!" Wanda understood the message.

"And requesting their permission to use the information. Again, because I have a bigger outreach than just us. That is part of your *Plan*." Christine and Wanda were mirrors for one another.

"That was a light bulb, thank you. I never thought about it that way. Recording a lecture would be one of the activities in the *Plan*."

"Right. You can just break that right down and put that in a spreadsheet or word processor. In the *Plan* you assign dates and deadlines to your dreams." Christine was a practical dreamer.

"Yes." Wanda could schedule the activities to bring her dreams to life.

"The *Plan* helps to refine your objectives. The objective of the book is to have the translations so that everyone—not just English speaking people—can understand this new idea that you have to share, that you've been given to share."

"It's very logical, you know? Sometimes I can get lost in terms of the *Plan*. I've got the vision, the heart, and the passion. But sometimes I don't see how approachable and reachable the *Plan* is."

"Well, I think you have a wonderful *Plan*, Wanda," Christine encouraged her.

"That was great!" Wanda was thrilled.

"I think things work out for the highest and best good of all because in the *Peace Process*, the *Plan* is for harmony. What better *Plan* than for you to live your dreams helping other people live theirs?"

"Yeah, right."

"And your dream is to have a spiritual practice where the value is recognized," Christine continued.

"Yes." Wanda agreed.

"What would a spiritual practice be without recognition of the value of it?" Christine asked the obvious question.

"Exactly, you're right," Wanda smiled.

"So, that is the whole point—to recognize the value of doing things with a heart."

"It is priceless, it really is," Wanda nodded.

"A real treasure," Christine confirmed.

"And I would never mistreat someone in terms of the price that I put on my service or what I want to share," Wanda added.

"Even pennies will add up because it will be shared with so many people. That's how the school and the institute will manifest, because everybody will contribute. You could offer an online course so there is not a lot of overhead, you know?" Christine asked.

"Oh, yeah!" Wanda had been looking into mentoring a class on the Internet.

"The student accepts the next module that fits into their schedule. You've written it once and it is in the book. Now people are downloading the module as they come to their spiritual purpose and are ready for the next, it's already done."

Christine grasped more details out of the ether. "Perhaps it is twelve audio lessons, which are in the book and in the workbook, so there is a lot of reinforcement. Even if people came to the institute, it could be an online place. The money needs to go into the place where you will be teaching, so that people can come to you—or perhaps you could travel and spread that good method."

"I think there is something, would you agree that part of the *Plan* what I am hearing you say, is yes, you can have workbooks, you can have online courses, but at the same time ultimately part of my *Plan* is the face to face gathering, the power in the gathering of the individuals?" Wanda searched Christine's face for her reaction.

"Yes, both. Absolutely," Christine was quick to agree.

"That's really what you've been talking about, that you need both," Wanda observed as Christine took the yellow *Plan* sign from her.

"Yes, Wanda, be open to that," Christine said as she gave her a new placard.

6.5   LOVE IS THE ANSWER

"What we're going to do now is *Work* for harmony. *Work* is the fourth step in the *Peace Process*, and the color for *Work* is green. I know you will identify with green, which is a symbol of growth that is associated with Mother Nature. Spring has sprung and the *Work* we are going to do is, as you know, of a mental nature—meaning that the true spiritual work happens in the thought of it."

"That's very powerful what you just said," Wanda held up her right hand motioning Christine to stop. "The true spiritual work happens . . ."

"With the thought of it. It's already done and that is where it begins and ends. As we flow that into the world, we get to see it. And that's like the Mother Nature. We get to see the beauty of Father Sky and Mother Earth working together to create the greenery and the forest. They work together. Without the air there would be no exchange between nature and people. Trees give us the oxygen and we give them . . ." Christine searched for the right word.

". . . carbon dioxide!" Wanda chimed in.

"So, it's very much that we are all working together. Not just on a human level. This is a planetary thing because, spiritually speaking, Mother and Father are conscious, and we are their children. We have been given an inheritance that we would like to spend wisely. So, our *Work* is simply for you to get comfortable, put down your sign, and go into a meditation."

"Okay." Wanda uncrossed her legs and placed her feet flat on the floor.

"My gift to you is to have you close your eyes and take a nice deep breath and then a big exhale with an audible *ahh*. Inhale again and fill up your lungs. Let that expand your chest. Exhale one more *ahh*. And the third breath as you inhale, let your shoulders rise up so you can get a big expansion and let me hear you say *ahh* . . ."

"*Ahh* . . ." Wanda laughed and wore a big smile as she let go.

"Yes. Be comfortable. Just relax." Christine paused to let Wanda settle into the silence.

"In the guided meditation, you will send love to this injustice that we have uncovered as being nothing more than a misperception, a little twist on the truth. Know in your heart, that the money is nothing, that the spirit is everything. But in the material world, the value of the spirit must be translated, and it is all right to make the translation. To see our spirit as being bigger than us, we want to reach out to more people in different languages, cultures, and faiths and not to be restricted or held back. We don't want to die with a blood clot in our body. And because we're all one body, then who is giving to whom?" Christine asked the question without expecting an answer.

"Let this misperception be uncovered as we hold it up to the sun and let the sun shine on it and dissipate the fog and the clouds so that we can see the dream. The dream is to share, to love, and to provide value for that which we hold so dear—all people everywhere. As we send this dream out into the spirit, the web, the matrix, we see that the spirit is already at work conspiring to make everything come true, because isn't it the highest and best good of all that this dream be realized?" Christine was in the spirit as she spoke.

"Isn't it your right, as a child of God to live what you came to do? Doesn't God share this dream with you, in his mind? Then be not afraid to take the value as the priceless treasure that you gave. Wanda, you are that treasure. You are a miracle. You are priceless. There is nobody that can afford to buy you. But you must find a way to put a price tag on your service and on your book so that you can cover the expenses of your school. This is an important part of your *Work*.

"See yourself as a teacher standing in front of the room. To inspire the class, Wanda, you have to believe in the value of your message. Recognize the risk of not discovering the value of what you teach—your students would be less than what they could be! The dream would be a headline and the story never written, and how tragic not to write the story of Dr. Wanda Bethea, and her research institute of learning with a heart." Christine delivered the message for Wanda with passion, and then she was silent.

"Now we thank God for his gift, which is to broadcast this message such that all the angelic realms surround you with a big hug and a kiss so that you will know that your dreams are realized in heaven. It's up to you to walk your destiny and they will see you when it is done. They are blowing kisses." Christine leaned over Wanda and blew her a kiss.

Feeling the air on her cheek made Wanda smile. "That was beautiful." Wanda wiped tears from her eyes.

"So, that is why you are here," Christine affirmed.

"Yes, thank you." Wanda put her hands together and clapped to show her appreciation.

6.6 WHAT DO YOU BELIEVE?

"Now that the *Work* is complete, now what?" Christine took the green sign from Wanda and handed her a blue one labeled *Measure*. "The fifth step in the *Peace Process* is *Measure*, and it is the discipline that you use to rate your meditation experience. The color for *Measure* is blue, which represents logic and truth. *Measure* provides feedback as you quantify how much love you felt in the meditation."

"All right." Wanda was thoughtful as she looked down at the blue sign she held in her hands.

"So, you get to *Measure*. How did you do in your meditation? Did you honestly send the love to your dream?" Christine wanted to know.

"I think I was there. Sometimes I waver. You know, there were moments when I know, and then I doubt. My faith is not as strong as it needs to be if my *Plan* is going to happen, if my vision is going to materialize. I think I'm still on the journey to make my faith stronger. If I could *Measure* it, sometimes I'm not totally convinced. I can see parts of it, I can see it and feel it, but there are a few clouds." Wanda waved one hand in the air as if to disburse the clouds that loomed over her head.

"Work on your trust of that spirit world, because you want the spirit as much as you want to share it. What you give is what you want to receive. And as much as you want to give people heart, spirit, and faith in unseen things, that is also what you want. So, you've got to trust—you've got to dis-cover your misperception. Offer that up to the sun and let those clouds dissipate."

Wanda nodded.

"Anything I have ever asked Jesus to do, he has done for me. Whether it was to start my car when it stalled on the highway. Or, when I had a carpet outside the studio and I really glued it down well and when it was worn out, I couldn't pull it up. I said 'In the name of Jesus, I want this carpet to come up!' A man came out from the restaurant next door and he said 'Can I help you?' I said, 'If you'll just pull up this corner, I'm sure I can get the rest.' Well, he pulled the whole carpet up and I wanted to thank him. So, I said 'I'm sorry, what is your name?' He said 'Jesse.' Close enough! Jesse, Jesus."

"Ahh," Wanda laughed with Christine at her folly.

"We ask for help to trust in things that we can't see, because we don't have the visibility—we're not supposed to. That's the gift of faith—trusting in what you don't see. If you believe it then you'll see it. It doesn't work the other way around."

"You don't see it and then believe it. You have to believe it first," Wanda agreed.

"And then you make it real by putting *Work* with your faith. In other words, there is real faith—you've got to believe it. There is you, there is the book, there are other people, and you can identify the cast of characters surrounding your dream. But the dream is really for you to live your spiritual nature and you want to do that by helping other people live theirs. What you give you will get because it's all the same thing—it's a closed circle. So, if you want to be spiritual, that's what you have to give and that's what you'll get— that's what you'll create. But, you must be constant in your faith. Tom says that when uncertainty is gone, so is opportunity. Think about that. Opportunity is created out of uncertainty. It's already done. It's decided—it's over. So, you want to move forward with the uncertainty—with the unknowns. Just bring them along, like a best friend. It's all right not to know, it's okay to move forward with uncertainty."

"It's amazing. I've often said that you don't have to know it all—you don't. It is okay to be uncertain."

"You don't have to know anything in order to love. Babies come into the world and they're just a bundle of love. What do they know? They have a clean slate."

"You don't have to know." Wanda shook her head.

"Love is the magnet that attracts everything to you. So, don't fall back and put up your little defenses—your doubts, and your fears, and your worries, because those are the clouds that keep you in the fog. Lift them up. It's okay that they are there and you recognize them, but you've got to lift them up, and they will disappear and then you move right through."

"Oh, you make it so beautiful! I can visualize it when you speak." Wanda smiled wistfully.

"That's good. I'm glad that you've measured that uncertainty. It's still there, but we've gone through the process of taking your faith, taking the uncertainty and disrobing it. What's it covering up? Is it covering up a blood clot? Let's thin that blood and move it on because we don't want to be backed up in our spiritual body. We are one body—we are one! So, you are just doing your little part to help the whole."

6.7   CELEBRATE THE JOURNEY

"All right Wanda and now, as the grand finale, you get to *Value* this whole process and the progress you've made today," Christine said as she traded the light blue sign for a dark blue one. "The *Value* discipline is the sixth step in the *Peace Process*. The color for *Value* is indigo, which denotes spiritual development and fulfillment. Now, tell me how you valued the time that we just spent."

"Oh, I learned so much. I'm very grateful for this opportunity today to share and for what you've taught me. You have reaffirmed, repeated, and reiterated what I know. Sometimes I need to hear it and see it more than once or twice. You revitalized and renewed— oh, the vision, the vision! My heart was palpitating really fast when you said 'the book is done, tell us what's in the book.' Wow!" Wanda expressed her gratitude.

"And you did! I was amazed at how easy it was for you to describe the contents of the book." Christine knew the book lived in Wanda's heart. "That was very powerful. The book's already done. Just bring it down. It's already done and it will manifest at the right time."

"That's what I valued. Wow—you took me right there. Right there, so I was clear. And I liked—I valued the notion of dis-cover to uncover, uncover, uncover. And the *Work*, the *Work* is already done, and that is where the heart is. But it has to be with love, it has to be with love," Wanda said, reflecting on the lessons she learned from their *Peace Process* session.

"Anything done with love is of the spirit, because the spirit is love. When you flow your river of love, it doesn't matter what you do. It doesn't matter how much you take from somebody or how much you give to somebody else because your arms are open. You take, and you give, and it just flows through you." Christine stood with arms wide and hands open.

"That's a beautiful image." Wanda extended her arms out. "That's a teaching!" she exclaimed smiling. "That's a teaching. So, that's what I valued, the teaching today. Feeling joy—there was joy, that's why I cried. Tears of joy and I could just feel joy all around me," Wanda laughed. "Thank you. It's peaceful, a peace-full feeling."

"I think of peace as the by-product of sending love, like the ashes from a burning log. Peace is a residual of having loved. And you can't buy it, and you can't get it from somebody else because it comes from you—it's a giving of your self."

"So, that's what I valued. I *Value* this whole process and the teaching is beautiful. Thank you for that."

"And I thank you for being my friend, Wanda. You know, whenever you teach this process, you learn as much as you teach. The teaching is not only for you, but because it's of the spirit, it is also for me and so I accept the teaching from you, and from the spirit. So, thank you." Christine turned to face the video camera. "And thanks for being with us. Have a great day!"

"Yes, a peaceful day," Wanda added, looking up at the camera.

"Peace be unto you always." Christine concluded the session.

6.8   EXERCISE

1.   Describe your life's purpose.

2.   What are you doing to fulfill your life's purpose?

3.   Create the future headline for an article that tells your success story. What does the article say about you?

7

Envision Peace

In my dream, the angel shrugged and said,
If we fail this time, it will be a failure of imagination
& then she placed the world gently
in the palm of my hand.

—Brian Andreas

It was Barbara who had helped Christine envision peace with her stepson by leading her through the *Peace Process*. At that time Christine struggled with her own family crisis. Ryan was almost nineteen years old and still living at home. His bedroom was his domain, and he was fond of electronics, which he often picked up at garage sales. Christine began to worry that the condition of his room was the reason their Indialantic house was not selling. When the real estate agent recommended that the price of their home be dropped further, Christine turned to her dear friend Barbara for help. Within three months Ryan cleaned his room, enrolled at college, and the real estate agent, Joy Tamburr, sold the house for a fair price.

7.1   WHAT TAKES YOUR PEACE?

Two years later, Barbara asked Christine to guide her through the *Peace Process* for her own personal dilemma. Christine was happy to return the favor and she invited Barbara over. When Barbara arrived at AquaTerra, Christine had prepared for their session by placing a box of tissues and a glass of water near the chair in her office. Barbara made herself comfortable in the black leather chair and kicked off her sandals as Christine turned the video camera on to capture their dialogue and Barbara's expressions.

Christine began, "We are here today with Dr. Barbara Hodal, who is a dear friend. She has offered to help me record a video of our *Peace Process* session. I really believe that the video is going to be useful, Barbara—to you personally. You will be able to remember some of the important things that we've said."

"As you know, the Six-Discipline Model of the mind flows from *Discover*, *Envision*, *Plan*, *Work*, *Measure*, and to *Value* like a rainbow river of light. The Six-Discipline Model is like a computer program that processes any thought with functional inputs and outputs. The *Peace Process* is one thought of peace in just six simple steps," Christine explained as she stood beside the video camera.

Christine gave Barbara a clipboard with a pen. "Here is a diagram of the *Peace Process*. I know you've seen this before, but here it is again in case you want to take any notes. Do you have any questions as we begin your journey to peace of mind?" Christine asked.

"Hmm, I don't think so, Christine," Barbara said as she put the clipboard down on the floor.

Christine handed Barbara a red sign with the word *Discover* on it in two-inch gold letters. "Let's begin with the discipline *Discover*. If you'll just hold this sign, it will let viewers know that we're in the *Discover* discipline. Hopefully, we're going to uncover some form of injustice, since you've come for the *Peace Process* because something is taking your peace. As you can see, the color for the sign is red and that's because we start with your fears, worries, and concerns. What you will talk about in this session will be up to you. It should be something that is close to your heart— either a big question that you have or some situation that causes you stress. Can you think of anything that you would like to work on today?"

Barbara tossed back her blonde curls as she spoke. "Yes, I would like to work on my debt, and where I'm at with that right now."

"All right, and where are you at with that right now?" Christine asked.

"Pretty deep!" Barbara held her breath and let out a hearty laugh to break her tension.

"Okay, that's why we're here, right?" Christine asked gently.

"I do know that it's temporary, but I'm not in a peaceful place about it," Barbara explained.

"It's really bothering you," Christine restated.

"Yeah, it is," Barbara admitted.

"So, let's take a look at your feelings surrounding the debt. Tell me how they weigh on your shoulders. Can you think of an example?" Christine asked.

"Well, for one thing, I think the biggest effect I'm feeling is that my freedom is restricted. Even though I've got credit cards, I realize I can't keep buying on credit. I have to start paying things off. Right now, I'm 'robbing Peter to pay Paul.' I feel like for a long time I had things under control and it wasn't a big deal. Now, I'm overwhelmed."

"Are you seeing this as a limitation? Because you know you are an unlimited being," Christine reminded Barbara.

"Yes, I know that in my heart," Barbara nodded. "But that's not how I feel right now."

"This limitation is not the way you want to perceive yourself. Now you have a liability, and there's an actual dollar amount that you have to pay back," Christine continued.

"Right. Exactly. That's exactly it," Barbara agreed. "It does have to be paid back. I know that."

"Absolutely," Christine confirmed.

"It's not just going to disappear." Barbara was realistic.

"Right." Christine said.

"I don't want to think about bankruptcy." Barbara frowned. "I've always had great credit and I've always been very responsible. I do know that my financial situation is temporary and, for a long time, it was manageable for me. But, it's getting more and more difficult for me to live with every day and that's where I'm starting to really lose my peace. I worry now, about how I will keep my head above water. I've thought about going back to Virginia and opening a chiropractic office. That would give me some type of steady income so I could start paying off my debt. I'm also open to the universe sending it to me in some form or another—but until that happens . . ."

"Barbara, I know you are a positive thinker, but it's okay to understand what makes you feel afraid. And, that's what we're going to look at right now. Let me ask you—what's the worst that could happen in your situation? What is the worst that could happen to you surrounding this debt?" Christine asked gently.

"I guess the worst that could happen is that I can't pay the money back and that I will have to declare bankruptcy." Barbara looked worried.

"And, then what would happen?" Christine pursued the fear.

"Well, then your credit rating is shot all to hell." Barbara suddenly remembered the video recording. "Oops, sorry," she apologized to the camera equipment.

Christine, still standing beside the video camera, grinned at her friend.

Barbara continued. "You know what? When that happens, I really don't know what that would mean. Do you lose all your credit cards? You know, at least one credit card is essential if you want to fly anywhere or if you have to rent a car. There are so many things that you can't do unless you have a credit card."

Christine nodded sympathetically.

"I don't know what the process is with declaring bankruptcy and I don't really want to do it for a lot of different reasons—not just the credit card thing. Yet, part of me feels like it would just be easier to do that. But, I also feel like I got myself into this situation and it's my responsibility to get myself out." Barbara sighed, anxiously twirling her hair with a finger. "I'm open to the universe taking care of it for me, whether it's by winning the lottery, receiving an inheritance, or all my creditors disappearing. I'm just starting to get really worried." Barbara expressed her concerns.

"Barbara, you and I both know that worry brings more of the same—that's really why you're here. You already know that this is a call for love, and I hear your call. I have been through bankruptcy myself, so I can tell you what happens. After bankruptcy, you're still who you've always been, which is a child of God. There isn't anything you can do to take away from who you really are—or from the love that is always present for you."

Barbara listened intently.

Christine continued, "There are lessons in bankruptcy such as *you are not your money*. I guess some of us just have to go through that in order to get that lesson. I do see that you've given up a successful chiropractic practice for something else that has given you debt. Let's talk about what you have now that you didn't have before," Christine prompted Barbara.

"Well, sure." Barbara nodded. "I'm definitely further along on the spiritual path knowing now, as you mentioned—who I really am. You can lose your idea of who you are, but you can't lose who you really are—because you are a child of God always."

Barbara continued. "I've learned a lot in these last two years taking courses. I've grown tremendously and I'm grateful for that. I know that the more I worry, the more it expands. I do know my situation is temporary and it's not who I am. The contrast makes me clear that I want to be as free as God created me. I desire complete financial freedom, whatever that entails. I would like to be in a position to help if my family or friends need anything. I also want to take more classes to further develop myself. So, I do know what I want." Barbara picked up the glass of water and took a sip.

7.2   THE PATH OF OPPORTUNITY

"Well, I think you are already on to the next path, which is the opportunity to see the positive aspects of your situation. I'm already hearing that you want to be responsible for the debt that has been accumulating. The benefit to you is a new consciousness and you can use that awareness to help other people," Christine summarized.

"Right," Barbara set her glass down on the end table.

"You were a good chiropractor, Barbara. Now, you'll be able to help people with back problems—and people with spiritual problems." Christine smiled.

"Yeah, that's a real benefit." Barbara nodded.

"You know that dis-ease comes from a spirit lacking peace and that can affect you physically."

"Right," Barbara approved. "We don't want that to happen."

"When you do your spiritual work, you free yourself. I see a real opportunity here for you to use this debt as the motivation to assist others—as you have been helped yourself." Christine expanded Barbara's vision.

"That's right," Barbara agreed. "That's exactly what I want to do. I've been given so much! I'm realizing and remembering that I am a divine child. I know, as you said, I am unlimited—I can help other people remember that as well. It wasn't that long ago that I was far from that level of consciousness. I really do want to be instrumental in leading people out of confusion and lifting them up." Barbara's expression was sincere.

"You are a master, Barbara. I know that you have gained the empathy required to help others who have lost their peace. You know how it feels to have the weight of the world on your shoulders. Having that experience has given you that empathy . . ."

"Hmm . . ." Barbara shut her eyes as she savored the thought.

". . . and how important it is that you allowed yourself this experience. Just take a look at how many of us are deeply in debt. Our country is, and on an individual basis, debt undermines peace of mind—like nothing else!" Christine was passionate.

"Hmm, right—we're not free anymore because of our obligations. I think that really is my point—that your freedom as a person to be able to come and go as you please, to have what you want and do what you want, is no longer there. And, you created it! So, there's the whole guilt thing—people saying 'you are smarter than that' and 'you shouldn't have done that' and 'what are you doing?' Blah, blah!" Barbara began to giggle.

7.3   PERSEVERANCE IS THE KEY

"As Americans, we all cherish our freedom. This country was built on freedom, and so terrorism aside, what has gotten us terrorized is our own debt and how do we get out of that? All right, this is how we do it in the *Peace Process*—we *Envision* a creative solution." Christine took the sign Barbara held and gave her a bright orange one.

"We know the worst-case possibility is for you to go bankrupt. You do realize that you're not your money and you already know that you are an unlimited being. So, bankruptcy is not a big deal except that you are responsible for the debt—and, spiritually, you're always accountable."

Barbara raised her eyebrows.

"So, there is really no getting out of that responsibility even if you think you're getting out of it. Let's choose to see this situation as an opportunity to give back what you've learned in your studies. Barbara, I want you to *Envision* the debt melting away by teaching what you've learned. Tell me how you're helping other people by sharing who you are now."

"Okay, because I'm very clear on that, Christine—I see it all the time!" Barbara threw her head back and laughed. "I could teach the steps that I have gone through in my transformation, and how I've changed as a result. I clearly see myself lecturing, teaching workshops, and signing books—showing people that in time and with perseverance they can realize their dreams, too." Barbara wore a big smile.

Barbara continued, "I can share my experience overcoming obstacles on the spiritual path—and how I got discouraged when my expectations were not met. My desires were probably this far away." Barbara held up her fingers an inch apart. "It's discouraging and frustrating when you acknowledge your fears, send them to the light, and think positive—and nothing seems to happen. I realize now that perseverance really is the key."

Barbara drew a deep breath. "I want to help others understand that if you keep doing the same thing, then you're going to get the same results. When you finally decide to do things differently, you will get new results!"

Christine grinned at her friend.

Barbara held the *Envision* sign with one hand as she gestured with the other. "I continue to grow and awaken to the gifts that I have been given—and those I'm entitled to as a child of God. I want to be a living example of how one awakens to the fact that there is no limit! We can have all that we desire because we are children of God and the universe is unlimited."

"You know, Christine—some things worth having take longer to develop. Looking back, I can see how I created obstacles that I had to break through. By having these experiences, I can share with other people, like you said, from an empathetic point of view. I want to teach perseverance knowing that God gives us what we ask for." Barbara smiled.

"Well, I love your dream, Barbara, and I know you will be the role model of self-discipline. Perseverance is a key spiritual practice because without it you won't walk through that next gate. So, perseverance might be your mantra as you move forward," Christine suggested.

Barbara nodded.

"Certainly that is what you're going to teach by sharing your experience. So, you've asked to teach a high and necessary spiritual skill and, perseverance, as you say, is the key," summarized Christine as Barbara returned the orange *Envision* placard.

7.4   EMPOWERED TO PROCEED

"You've just had a vision of what you'll be sharing to attain financial freedom. Let's *Plan* how you'll be empowered to proceed." Christine offered Barbara a yellow board with shiny gold letters.

"The *Plan* is always for harmony in the *Peace Process*. In this step, we'll assign resources such as people, time, and money to activities so that you can achieve your goal. So, let's schedule the workshop, write the first chapter of the book, or perhaps sketch the cover! Tell me how you're going to melt your debt, and when you're going to do it," Christine encouraged.

Barbara threw back her head and laughed. "Okay. That much I don't know. The vision is there. I just figured that the details and the necessary steps would reveal themselves in the proper time."

"You can think of me as a revealer of the next step because it is God's *Plan* that you have peace of mind." Christine smiled. "And you will know the *Plan* because it will give you feelings of love, joy, and happiness. Did you feel that as you declared your vision?" Christine asked.

"Mm-hmm," Barbara concurred.

"As a child of God, you are given free will to learn by your choices. You are free to extend God's love into the world. God's *Plan* for you is peace, love, and joy. And what would give that to you but for you to share your gifts? You will sing a song in your workshops, Barbara, that gives glory back to God," Christine assured her.

"Mmm . . ." Barbara was thoughtful.

"So, we're taking a look at which project you might work on that would bring you joy, give you happiness, and provide the money to pay your debt," Christine clarified.

"Okay, this might sound like it's not really a *Plan*, but it is. Uh, how do I word this?" Barbara searched her memory. "I remember taking one of those personality tests that indicated I am good at ideas and starting things, but then I tend to fizzle out. Seminar leaders talk about how easy it is to follow their program, and you see other people get it quickly—but I don't. I think that's been a pattern for me. My *Plan* of action right now is getting past my typical behavior." Barbara grimaced.

"One of the things that I've always wanted to do—and this may not seem related, but it's a perfect analogy—is to read faster with more comprehension. Well, I bought a book on speed-reading and I'm all for that, you know." Barbara laughed.

Christine listened patiently.

"But, I start reading this book and it describes what I need to do. So, I give it a try—and I walk away thinking *this is not helping me*. I need to change the way I read and I feel as though God is telling me to do things differently to get different results." Barbara flicked her curls back off her shoulder.

"If I continue to improve my comprehension I will have more clarity to own my God-given gifts. They will manifest more quickly and they will take shape on their own. Does that sound like a copout, Christine—if I just wait to see what happens?"

"Mm-hmm." Christine smiled. "So, what happens next?"

Barbara continued. "Well, as you know, I've been writing and recording my realizations over the past two years. It would be a good start if I transcribed and organized that information. That could be my game *Plan* right now. Christine, does that make sense?" Barbara asked.

"It does," Christine began slowly. "You're right. The next step is to *Plan*. Perhaps you need a little bit deeper understanding of God's *Plan* for your life."

Barbara nodded.

"You're already tuned into God's *Plan* through the material that has been given to you, and you must learn to trust that connection," Christine counseled her friend.

"Right, right," Barbara confirmed.

"There isn't anything more that you need to know. There is not a faster rate that you need to know it. You are already loved as much as you will ever be loved." Christine spoke softly.

"Your life is your gift from God. Free will is your gift from God. Your next breath is your gift from God. The *Plan* is your choice of how you will extend that love. The more that you can get yourself out of the way, the more pure that love is," Christine explained.

Barbara smiled.

"What is needed in the *Plan* is a commitment—in time, energy, and resources. You choose the vehicle. It could be a book. It could be a workshop. It could be anything!" Christine exclaimed.

"If you believe that time is of the essence—which song would you sing? Now, is it a book? A workshop? An inspirational message? Your *Plan* is about the important things you want to do to leave the world a better place because you were here."

"Right," Barbara agreed.

"You have an important lesson to impart. You can deliver your message like no one else can. When you trust your divine connection, you are given what you need to know," Christine reminded her friend.

"I'm looking in this step for the *Plan* that will realize your vision. It doesn't have to be done tomorrow. So, ask yourself: What do I need next? Who can help me? What resources do I have available? Then make your commitment to the *Plan*," Christine concluded.

7.5   I AM GOD'S HEALER

"Mm-hmm. The first part of the *Plan* is becoming a living example and I think I'm making progress through my writing and recording. I'm gaining the confidence to stand in front of a group of people. I'm not sure if teaching workshops or writing a book would be first," Barbara wondered.

"I would like to activate my chiropractic license in Virginia and to integrate Reiki, Angel Therapy, and Theta Healing within my practice. On the weekends, I can start teaching workshops about how to overcome barriers of discouragement and frustration. I'll write a book at the same time—and not wait for the book to be published. That is a *Plan* that I would like to see happen." Barbara began to map her route.

"Did I tell you, I saw Oprah deliver an inspirational speech at a televised conference? She spoke about how she was raised by her grandmother who always told her 'you are God's child.' Oprah said 'So, I knew *I am God's child, I am God's child, I am God's child*— and I claim all that entails!' She said it three times, just like that. And I understood she meant that, as God's child, she is entitled to

121

absolutely *everything* in God's kingdom. I was like *rock on, Oprah!*" Barbara exclaimed.

Christine laughed along with Barbara.

"Come on, and right then it was like, okay—own that *I am God's healer*. Christine, do you remember what an issue I had with that whole *God's healer* thing?" Barbara grinned.

"I sure do." Christine recalled Barbara's resistance.

"I'm claiming my oneness with God and my divinity. I'm not taking it away from anyone else. I've always said that I work for God. But you know, *I am God's healer*. Okay, I'm buying it now, God!" Barbara looked up and laughed. "I'm accepting it now, so I know it's going to come to fruition."

Christine smiled.

"I'm getting rid of my doubt and I'm going to stop comparing myself to others—I don't need to do that! God has lots of healers, but *I am God's healer*, so I have to claim that. For me, that is a huge step in this whole *Plan*." Barbara's face lit up.

"I would love, love, love not only lecturing and teaching—but healing. I have always wanted to contact Chiropractors Without Borders and sign up to serve overseas in villages where people need a doctor."

Barbara continued, "A lot of people don't understand that the chiropractic profession was founded on spiritual principles. I would love to be able to practice using the other healing modalities I have learned. And by claiming to be God's healer, I can go where I'm guided. I will be in a financial position to do healing work and spread God's love." Barbara beamed.

7.6   THERE IS A UNIVERSAL SUPPLY

"Yes, that's right, that is the *Plan!*" Christine exclaimed as Barbara gave her the yellow board. "The vibration in your heart will flow the *Plan* into your *Work*. So, what we'll do next is to breathe life into your wishes." Christine presented Barbara with the green sign labeled *Work*. "I'd like to take you through a guided meditation."

Barbara planted her feet on the floor and sat up tall in the chair. "Now, close your eyes, Barbara, and take a deep breath. Relax your shoulders gently down away from your neck," Christine instructed.

Barbara lowered her eyelids as she relaxed.

"Take another deep breath—this time from your toes—and let it fill up your lungs like balloons. As you exhale, feel the weight of worry lift off your shoulders." Christine spoke gently.

"I want you to know, trust, and believe that you are perfect, Barbara, just as you are right now. I want you to find the presence of God deep in your own heart space, which is your magnetic core. Connect to that source of infinite power," Christine said slowly.

"As you continue on your journey, you will choose which project to pursue. You may have several in various stages that you work on simultaneously—and that will depend on how you like to work. But, know that you do not need to wait until the slate is clean—or until the debt is met, to begin teaching the lessons that you have learned these past few years."

Christine continued, "There are students for you right now. Your credibility will come from your perseverance. You can show that you are beginning today to be responsible for your debt. You can tell your students that you have traded money in order to help them with the lessons that you've learned. Tell them that you chose your path to bring them a key spiritual practice—and that is perseverance." Christine paused.

"Your mind tricks you into thinking you're not good enough to stand up and share who you are. But, you can open your heart and speak your truth: *I love God. I'm God's child. I work for God. I'm God's healer.*" Christine put her hand over her heart.

"These words have deep meaning for me. They mean that God is there for me 24/7—even closer than my own breath—and God is there for you too, but you have to claim that for yourself. I know there is a universal supply and that whatever I declare, as a child of God, can come true. Maybe not on my time—on God's time. But, all you have to do is ask, Barbara, and I can tell you with certainty—you will receive," Christine assured her friend.

"You are a beautiful ray of light. And on that light beam you carry love for God and your fellow man—and the world, for trees, and for animals. Your song is the vibration deep in your heart that shares your love. As you sing your song, that song will lighten your load," Christine continued.

"It is time to begin to give back the gifts that you have gathered along your spiritual path. There are many. The more we give of ourselves, the more we demonstrate perseverance, courage, and commitment. Thank you, God, that we are able to walk together and erase that debt."

Barbara smiled, her eyes still closed.

"Tend to your field, cultivate it, and nurture it. Plant the seeds and let them grow. Be sure to water the soil and then be patient. When the seeds sprout forth, they will bear fruit and be harvested. Go in peace. Peace be with you always. I love you," Christine said softly. "Amen."

7.7   EVALUATE THE MEDITATION

"Now Barbara, when you're ready, you can open your eyes."

Barbara stretched her legs as her eyes opened.

"The next step in the *Peace Process* is *Measure*. Let's talk about what came up for you in the meditation." Christine traded the green sign for a blue one.

Barbara nodded. "It was awesome, very good. You are right—there are people I can teach right now. I love to teach. I need to be more serious about presenting my own workshops. I really enjoy seeing my friends soak up what I know. Many people are at that sponge stage—searching for spiritual guidance."

"So, in the meditation, you saw yourself giving workshops?" Christine wanted to know.

"Oh, definitely," Barbara agreed.

"Did you see yourself writing the book? I ask because I'm feeling that what came into your awareness is probably where you are meant to start. But, you'll have to sort through that. What else came up for you?" Christine wondered.

"I guess what I saw first was mainly the workshops. Through the workshops I can be a living example of an unlimited being—and I think that's how the whole book will come together. Does that make sense, Christine?" Barbara asked.

"Yes, it does," Christine confirmed.

"It makes sense in my head, but when I say it out loud, does it actually make sense to someone else?"

"The teaching and the questions that come out of the workshops all flow into the book. You will be the ultimate example of financial freedom, but that's not where you start the workshops. You start the workshops with owning your debt and then talking about perseverance—because that's how people will identify with you. Everyone faces challenges and by owning the debt you can help others face theirs," Christine said.

"Hmm . . ." Barbara smiled as she handed the blue placard labeled *Measure* to Christine.

7.8   APPRECIATING CLARITY AND DIRECTION

"Now let's *Value* the whole process, not just your meditation." Christine handed Barbara an indigo-colored sign.

"Okay, I'm not sure what you mean by that."

"The sixth step in the *Peace Process* is the *Value* you place on the hour we just spent together," Christine explained.

"Okay." Barbara was thoughtful.

"What's the wisdom that you're going to walk away with today?" Christine asked.

"Oh." Barbara wrinkled her brow.

"Like a summary wrap-up of our *Peace Process* session," Christine prompted.

"Well, it obviously made me more clear on what I want and need to do. With this whole process, I see how it's helpful—and why it's helpful to be empathetic. Very recently, I started—believe it or not—actually blessing the debt, and looking at it as a gift. I know now that losing my financial freedom is a lesson that taught me I want to be more than debt-free. I want to be able to manifest abundance and teach other people how to do that!" Barbara exclaimed.

"Very early in my chiropractic career I had a major challenge where I was in excruciating pain." Barbara recalled. "I couldn't even roll over—literally, I couldn't walk. I couldn't do anything—it was awful! It was the worst thing. But, I do remember I kept saying: *this will make me a better doctor; this will make me a better doctor . . .*"

The video recorder beeped, signifying that the hour-long session was over. "Well, Barbara, the video will be useful to help you recall your dreams and goals—and the commitments you made to be *God's healer.*" Christine smiled gently at her friend.

"Christine, I really can't thank you enough for your compassion! You have my permission to share our session so that others may benefit." Barbara stood up and gave Christine a big hug.

7.9   EXERCISE

1.   Empathy helps us identify with and understand another's situation and feelings. What experiences have you been through that help you to have empathy for others?

2.   We persevere by remaining true to our purpose in the face of obstacles or discouragement. Identify patterns of behavior that work for you. And, identify those that work against you.

3.   Your life is the opportunity to sing your song to your Creator. What song will you sing?

8

Plan for Inner Peace

Peace comes when we live in a spirit of love.

*To get along with others, we must love them
without forcing our love upon them. Imposing
our beliefs upon others will not bring peace.*

*To have concern for others, to respect their
rights and freedoms, and to let them
be themselves—this is peace.*

—Wynn Davis

"Christine has taken a huge step to the fulfillment of her dreams, and
we are proud to support her continued success through IBI Global,"
said Britt Allen at the local chapter meeting on Tuesday evening.
"She completed fifty hours of business skills training at the Free
Enterprise Forum in Los Angeles to become multiple venture
technology accredited. I'm pleased to present our speaker for
tonight, Dr. Christine." Britt smiled as she put her hands together
and the audience clapped politely with their Regional Manager.

During the networking meeting, Louis Gross introduced himself and said that he was new in town. Afterward, Christine gave Lou her business card. Lou called her later that week and explained that he needed help with some of the challenges he faced. Christine told him about the *Peace Process* and invited him over for a session. "Lou, bring a flower, a piece of fruit, or a candle as a love offering, and we'll see what we can do together."

8.1 HOW DO YOU FEEL?

Lou arrived at AquaTerra on a cool January morning in blue jeans and a brown turtleneck. "Hi, Lou." Christine greeted him at the door.

"Sixteen steps! Did you know there are sixteen steps up to your front door?" Lou gasped, offering her a big red apple.

"Oh, thank you!" Christine smiled, reaching for the apple. "Come on in."

"Thanks." Inside the two-story foyer, Lou took off his sneakers and left them on the tile floor.

"We'll be working in my office—there's the door to the bathroom," Christine pointed across the spacious room. "Lou, why don't you get comfortable in that chair?"

"Okay." Lou settled into the black leather chair.

"The *Peace Process* begins with your passion, Lou," Christine said as she pressed the record button on the video camera. "Let's start with what's in your heart." She handed Lou the red sign for the *Discover* discipline. "Tell me how you feel right now."

"Sick—physically, very sick. Exhausted, frightened, worried, and very confused—and overwhelmed and angry. I don't have very much physiology to control how I am. I need to get more focused on what I'm supposed to be doing. I'm not well enough to do that and things keep going downhill. So, I don't know how to get out of it," Lou muttered.

"Let's start by taking a deep breath, Lou. Just inhale now—and then exhale very slowly. We're going for a nice balanced breath, so close your eyes and breathe from below your belly button," Christine said, her voice soft.

Behind the heavy dark frames of his glasses, Lou closed his eyes.

Christine continued, "Let the air fill your lungs and expand them like balloons. As you exhale, I want you to relax and let your shoulders come down and fall away from your neck."

Lou held the *Discover* sign with two fists, his tension obvious.

"Now, Lou, take another deep breath. Draw this one up from your toes, if you can. Let the breath fill your body and lift your head. As you exhale, imagine that the sun is shining down on your shoulders. God is here for you," Christine said gently.

Lou gave a slight nod.

"Take another breath and let it move through all your internal organs. Think of your lungs as big party balloons. It's your birthday, Lou—we're going to celebrate your birthday today. You're going to be a new Lou. Every day is a new day to be a new you. Now, exhale and relax," Christine coached.

Lou sat back in the chair and crossed his ankles.

"Let's take one more deep breath, and with this breath fill up from the Holy Spirit, knowing that you have access to an infinite well of resources. And as you exhale, let all the demons flow out of your body—just let them go."

Christine watched as Lou seemed visibly relieved.

"When you're ready, you can open your eyes," Christine said slowly.

Lou lifted his eyelids. "That really helped."

"Yeah," Christine agreed, handing him a glass of water. "Let's talk about what's taking your peace, Lou. Why are you so mad?"

"Because I've ruined my life—and wasted my life." Lou squinted.

"And how did you do that?" Christine asked.

"In a lot of ways. I didn't take advantage of opportunities that were offered to me. I didn't pay attention when people told me to take care of myself. And I didn't stay in a place where I could make more money and be in a spiritual practice." Lou shook his head. "It's been one thing after another . . ."

"Mm-hmm." Christine nodded.

"I really don't know how to get back on track. I don't know how to make myself better. I don't have any resources here—except for the Veterans Administration, where my doctor gives me oxygen three times a week. And, when I go there, the gasoline for my car is expensive," Lou grumbled.

Christine listened carefully.

"All my ideas about what I could do this year—they all fell flat. No air in my balloon! I even had a psychic tell me that two years ago," Lou recalled.

"My retirement account is way down, I'm not able to work, and my disability doesn't cover enough. People who said they would help me are not. I don't have the physical well-being and the money to make myself better, or to go on the gigs that people are offering me—so, it all seems hopeless." Lou paused.

Christine stood silently beside the camera.

"The short term is not hopeless, because I can get out of bed and spend money. I take more money out of my retirement and go to the health food store and get juices and that makes me feel better. Last night I had a lot of juice. I went to church, where they had classes in a big auditorium with good air. The good air helped me breathe better than I have in months. I felt calm and connected, because I had all that spiritual energy around me," Lou continued.

"I need to live in a place with good energy and be able to breathe and build myself back up. My fantasy is to go back to the Zen Meditation Center in Los Angeles where I used to live. I'd like to live at the ashram again—and chant and forget about everything else. But, my guides keep saying no." Lou sighed.

8.2 OPPORTUNITY LIVES NOW

"That's probably enough," Christine said slowly. "Lou, you have a great awareness of what you don't want. You know what you don't want, which is an opportunity for you."

"It doesn't do me any good." Lou shook his head.

"In the *Peace Process* we *Discover* the down side and the up side of the possibilities. Opportunity is the good possibility in the present moment. I heard you say that you want to live in a place with spiritual energy. You want to chant and meditate. So, you just made a shift from the negative to the positive."

"Yeah, sure." Lou nodded.

"And that's what you want," Christine said simply.

"Mm-hmm," Lou agreed.

"Repeating that experience is not only in your awareness, but it's in your ability—you already know where to go," Christine reminded Lou.

"Every single person that I talk to these days says exactly what you're saying. My acupuncturist said it just two days ago. The pastor said it in church last night. This morning somebody on the phone was giving me a spiritual healing and said it."

"Right, so what does that tell you, Lou?" Christine asked.

"But, I'm so exhausted," Lou complained.

"Even though change can be a scary thing," Christine continued, "it can still happen for you because you know what you want. You have the opportunity to go to a place to rest and rejuvenate."

"Not really, money-wise," Lou contradicted.

"Suppose you went anyway. Could you trust that the money you needed to stay would show up?" Christine asked.

"Go to LA and get clients?" Lou sounded doubtful.

"Well, as you help others, you may find your own healing."

"But, I'm not getting any clients in this area," Lou complained.

"Maybe you're not meant to, Lou. Perhaps that is the motivation to move you where you're truly meant to be."

"Christine, are you suggesting that I'm not going to stay here? I should go some place else? Is that what you're saying? Am I translating right?"

"I'm just mirroring. I'm reflecting what your intuition is telling you." Christine felt Lou's frustration.

"Okay," Lou allowed.

"Because, you know best. You are sharing with me what you don't want and you are very clear, Lou. You have a brilliant mind."

"My intuition is very good. I often know before I go somewhere what will happen. But, I'm tired of being so sick." Lou grimaced.

"It's all right to be at the bottom, because as far down as you go, you can also soar that high," Christine said confidently.

"It hasn't worked like that for me," Lou reminded her.

"Hmm, you can be patient and know that what goes down must come up." Christine was optimistic.

"Not necessarily," Lou argued. "Sorry for being so negative. I'm not supposed to be talking like this. But, I'm tired of being Pollyanna! I'm tired of telling everybody—a shrink, a doctor, a therapist, clients, or anybody else—yes, this is good, this is this way, and this is that way. I'm tired of it, okay?" Lou's tone of voice expressed his aggravation.

"There's no need to apologize, Lou. Let's spend some time talking about what you like to do," Christine suggested.

Lou sat back and took a deep breath.

"Well, I like when I can help people—to be kind and caring. I like when people bring me their problems. I felt good when a massage therapist from Kansas called me about one of her clients with serious back problems. I was able to use my Back-Fix Bodywork techniques and I know that therapy helped. I like doing my thing. My astrologer in New Mexico said that's what I should do. As I talk to you about liking to do my own thing—my body relaxes!" Lou grinned.

8.3   WHAT MAKES YOU HAPPY?

"Ahh, then let's *Envision* what your dream is." Christine took the sign Lou held and gave him the bright orange one. "Lou, what are you doing when you feel happy?"

"What makes me happy?" Lou paused. "Well, I see myself standing in front of a group of people, teaching them about my techniques and I feel myself smiling. I've pictured this in my mind many times. You know, I've already produced stretching videos for athletes, and I could create more to target different markets." Lou beamed.

"So, you're a teacher," Christine observed.

"Exactly. In fact, I had a psychotherapist who does astrology, and years ago she gave me a reading over the phone. She said 'I see all these planets in the second house, in the fifth house, and in the seventh house. I see you as a teacher and a writer.' So, that's how I knew," Lou explained.

"When I massage people, I sing to them as I do the deep tissue work: *It's in the fascia, it's in the fascia, da-da, la-la, ta-da!* Everybody laughs, but they all remember, and we have a good time. I'm doing heavy stuff on their body by bringing out their emotional trauma—and singing makes it lighter. People have more fun and I have more fun." Lou grinned from ear to ear.

"Your speaking voice does have a great quality," Christine noticed.

"Really? I always thought it was too nasal. But, I used to work on it through guided relaxation for clients when I lived at the Zen Center. One guy who came in was so frazzled I put him in shivasana. I said *relax your toes and your toenails . . . loosen between your toes . . . relax the bones of your toes . . . and in-between the bones of your toes.* I had it on tape. When I started doing acupressure with the energy work, I found people relaxed even more. At the end of the session, I would play *Chariots of Fire* and different pieces of music to open their chakras!" Lou exclaimed.

Christine laughed with Lou.

"I can do release therapy worldwide over the phone," Lou continued. "I worked with a woman in southern Florida for a number of hours doing emotional trauma release. As a child, her father sexually abused her and she repressed the fact that her mother had ignored the situation. She had also been raped as a teenager and feared for her life. I was able to release all of these things and a lot of past-life stuff."

"Yes, I can see how you might have helped her release that trauma, because your voice has a command and a presence that made her feel safe."

"Really?" Lou was surprised.

"Absolutely," Christine confirmed.

"God, Christine. That's worth the price of admission right there!"

"When you make others feel safe they are free to open up to you. With your commanding voice, you can steer people in positive ways because of your empathy," Christine explained.

"Yes, I have a lot of empathy. Every time I have a big physical crisis in my own life, I have more compassion for others and their difficulties," Lou nodded.

"It's not by mistake that you had so many setbacks. You are a master, Lou—and you've chosen your path. Your heart has been tenderized as a result of many wounds—and that allowed you to help this woman."

"Oh." Lou was thoughtful.

"Absolutely," Christine repeated.

"My friend called and said she's most attracted to me when I'm doing my spiritual practice. My concentration gets better when I practice. I've been chanting at the Yoga Shakti Mission every night for over a week. Last Sunday, Mataji started talking to me about doing my work. She came over to me so kindly and put her hand on my head like a grandmother. It really struck me, you know?"

"Yeah, hands are a symbol of work and responsibility. I'm sure her hands have a healing touch," Christine said as she took the *Envision* placard from Lou.

8.4   A PROMOTIONAL VIDEO

"That brings us to the *Plan*." Christine handed Lou the yellow sign. "Lou, how can we put resources of people, time, and money into a *Plan* for you to realize your vision of helping others?"

"Yeah, you tell me." Lou grinned.

"We'll work it together," Christine suggested.

"I have some ideas," Lou offered.

Christine smiled. "Okay, let's hear them."

"I don't know what will work—so, I'm just going to put out a bunch of things."

"And I'm going to mirror them back to you."

"First, I'll talk about bodywork."

"Okay, bodywork," Christine echoed.

"My clients are serious athletes who feel tight and need to stretch. I could write a book about my techniques and sell it with the stretching video on my website," Lou began.

"How about making a video that promotes your work? Say you *Plan* a thirty-second video for your website. Perhaps the first five seconds might be about bodywork for athletes. Then, Lou, tell me what you might include in the next five seconds of your promotional video," Christine prompted.

"Another idea is helping people who are injured with some sort of back pain. My housemate said, 'Lou, I've had the best people in LA work on me and you have better hands.' A friend of mine from Sedona said, 'Lou, your hands are golden.' I did a trade with another friend and she said, 'Ooh, I had forgotten about those hands.' I know I'm digressing," Lou confessed.

"So, we see your hands streaming light in the video?" Christine asked.

"Well, they do—when I work, my hands get hot!" Lou exclaimed.

"The *Plan* is to create a thirty-second video, and we have five seconds for athletes who need to stretch. We've got five seconds of healing hands for those with back pain. Lou, what else is in your video?"

"I can show how I help people go through trauma release— and it's easy to do the way I was trained. If I could train somebody else to do it on me, I'd be happier than a pig, you know?" Lou chuckled. "Oh, I've got to tell you. Remind me before I go to tell you the pig joke."

"Okay." Christine smiled.

8.5   ENERGIZE YOUR DREAM

"It's like things pop up out of nowhere, Christine. When I was in Salt Lake City, a woman was referred to me and she had a tight neck. The woman was very hyper, very tense. She could pay me only a small amount, but I found out her daughter had been killed by a hit-and-run driver ten years earlier. I had her sit sideways on a stool, and I worked on her back, her neck, her head, and her arms," Lou recalled.

Christine listened intently.

"I had her lie down and worked on her head some more, worked on the chest and the shoulders a little bit. I said okay, now you're structure is opened enough so we can do release processing. From there, we worked down into the belly and pelvis, where a lot of anger started coming up. I had her kicking, and then she got into the deep sorrow in the heart organ itself. It took us three hours—that's a long session!" Lou exclaimed.

"I'll tell you Lou, we need to get you back to *Work* so now we're going to do a guided . . ."

Lou interrupted. "Oh, and the last thing I didn't tell you is I've got to teach this. That's the big thing because that's where I can make money."

"Well, that's where your value is," Christine observed.

"Sure, and I need agents. Remember in the networking meeting Britt said if you're not a genius at it, have somebody else do it."

"If it's not your genius, it's not your job," Christine clarified.

"Okay, I know what to say in marketing and how to make flyers so they look great. I have four or five different programs that people can use to train on my website. I want to do videos of energy release stuff. But, I need people to market me and put me in touch with influential people. And I need to get really healthy so I can do all this." Lou waved his hand as he spoke.

"You know, I have a website—backfixbodywork.com."

"The website will have your testimonials?" Christine asked.

"Oh, I already have testimonials up the wazoo on my website from the world record-holder in the long jump, the world record-holder in the triple jump, and the six-time British women's middle distance champion."

"Now I'm going to guide you in a meditation so we can energize your dream. When you're ready, Lou, make yourself ʻnfortable and close your eyes."

Lou took off his glasses. "Can I go to the bathroom first?"

ʼs, of course, you can!" Christine smiled.

8.6 HOW YOU HEAL

"We are back, and Lou is getting comfortable for the guided meditation," Christine spoke to the video camera as she handed Lou the green placard labeled *Work*. "Lou, I'm going to ask you to close your eyes and take a nice deep breath to fill your lungs. As you exhale, relax and sink into that cozy chair."

Lou sat back in the chair and drew another breath.

"In our mind's eye, we can see the *Work* that Lou is doing. On the Internet there are testimonials from world-class athletes, an individual who suffered a back injury, and a mother who lost her precious child years ago. These people are grateful to you, Lou, for your soothing voice and healing hands. As your hands shine their light, you help to make this world a better place."

Lou uncrossed his ankles and planted both feet on the floor.

"Lou is here with empathy and healing skills that come from lifetimes of study, meditation, and prayer. He had to go to the bottom of the deepest pit that he might meet others on the path and share his light with them. As Lou emerges from his dark night, we can see that he is ready to teach. Not only to help those in need, but to educate others that his *Work* may live on as a legacy of love."

Lou's palms lay relaxed on his jeans.

"God wishes to put his hands on Lou's shoulders and remind Lou that he is always there as a helper and a lover of humanity. So, Lou, all you need to do is ask and you will receive—not on your time, but on God's time. Be patient because God's delays are not denials! He is with you and so is Jesus Christ. And, if you ask in his name, you are sure to receive that which you need to help others."

Christine continued. "You will be miraculous in your healings because God is pleased to perform a miracle as you share your love. Indeed, the miracle is your love and is the love of God through you. So, don't be confused who does the real healing—it is the Holy Spirit coming through you! As you step aside, there will be miracles."

Lou bowed his head, showing gray in his thick brown hair.

"This is your *Work* to do this lifetime and we now know where your focus needs to be. The video is a tool that you can use to replay what you have been shown today—but the message will remain the same. You have become clear about your *Work*. And, your healing of others is, of course, how you heal yourself."

Christine paused. "God thanks you, the angels thank you, and I thank you for your *Work*, because it is needed—and it is needed now. We love you and we are always here for you—closer than your next breath," Christine said softly. "Be well then. Be at peace. God bless you! Amen."

8.7   SITTING IN MEDITATION

"When you are ready Lou, you can open your eyes."

Lou blinked as he handed Christine the *Work* placard.

"Now, you can *Measure* how you did." Christine gave Lou the blue sign to hold. "Since I wasn't inside your head, just tell me what happened to you. What did you do during the meditation?"

"Well, when you were talking I was mostly listening to you."

"And . . ."

"I wasn't thinking about doing the *Work*, but I was thinking about being at the Zen Center in Los Angeles."

"Ahh, that's coming up for you very strongly."

"And I just wanted to meditate a lot—it's what I feel comfortable doing. When you said 'Jesus' it struck me—because I do have that connection."

"Of course. Well, he is here in the room. If you look, you can see him. Do you see him now?"

"Oh, I see the poster—but I thought you meant his spirit."

"I sense the master is there for you," Christine nodded. "So, the Zen Center came up again. What else? Anything else pop into your head?"

"I was sitting in meditation," Lou reflected as he put his glasses back on.

"Maybe you could teach that. There are many people that need to learn inner strength from stillness. Would you be willing to teach that and hold classes?"

"Yeah, if I'm living at the Zen Center, I won't have to worry about that—that's what they do there."

"Right!" Christine grinned.

147

"I would rather live and practice at the Zen Center and go to other meditation centers and practice. In my mind, I picture selling everything and getting the money to go back to LA. I don't know if the universe is going to say 'yes' but, those are my ideas."

"Well, I can tell you one thing. You said 'yes' to the Zen Center, because that's what came up when you were relaxed."

"I don't know about smog," Lou worried.

"Well, I don't know either, but your heart is there so perhaps you create a Zen Center somewhere else. I do know your heart is in that practice."

"That's what my life is about." Lou nodded.

8.8   SOMEBODY LISTENED

"Lou, let's talk now about the *Value*." Christine traded Lou the light blue sign he held for the dark blue one labeled *Value*.

"The decisions I've made went against my long-term values and I assume that's because I've been physically and mentally drained," Lou began.

"You thought you didn't have options?" Christine guessed.

"No, I had options, but I chose the wrong things," Lou explained.

"Okay." Christine nodded.

"I didn't listen to the right people, I didn't have faith, and I gave my power away. That's where I still am—having trauma and feelings of terror every single day," Lou expressed.

"How about the *Value* of this *Peace Process* session. What did you get out of it? Is there any new knowledge or guidance that you're going to walk away with today?"

"I was able to talk about my thing in an organized way," Lou nodded.

"Yes, you did. It was very clear," Christine agreed.

"That was very good. So, each time I have the chance to talk about this, I feel more organized."

"You can also transcribe the video," Christine suggested.

"And, somebody listened to me—that was very important."

"Hmm."

"I'm still seemingly fighting a whole lot of it single-handedly, okay? My long-term finances and credit are washed out—I don't even have the money to spare for bankruptcy! It all happened in a giant cataclysm of bad decisions and going the wrong way."

"Mmm."

"Astrologically, I have intercepted signs. That's because I didn't make good choices in a previous lifetime. All I have to give people right now is these hands and my talents. If I could get myself healthy—that's the whole question that has been going on for years." Lou winced.

"Yeah, you know that's the end of our *Peace Process* session," Christine sighed. "You have a lot to be grateful for, Lou. And Lou, I am grateful to you for reminding me of a famous quote by Jim Rohn—*Discipline weighs ounces, while regret weighs tons.*"

In the chair, Lou stretched out his legs as he handed Christine the *Value* sign.

"Hey, Lou, before you go—won't you tell me the pig joke so we can laugh one more time?"

8.9   EXERCISE

1.   What makes you happy?

2.   We become self-reliant when we seek our own inner guidance. Give an example of a time when you made a conscious choice, and when you gave your power away.

3.   Negative thinking either criticizes, condemns, or complains. Share something you don't want to happen. Turn it around and become aware of what you really do want.

9

A Habit of Love

The fruit of the Spirit is love, joy, peace.

—Galatians [5:22]

"Welcome everyone to the *Peace Process*. We are here today with Reverend Audrice Collins." Christine faced the camera with a smile in a violet shirt and white linen slacks.

"Glad to be here," Audrice called out from the burgundy leather recliner in Christine's bedroom on the third floor at AquaTerra.

"Instead of being videotaped herself, Audrice prefers audio only, so I'll be the one on camera for this hour-long session because it's helpful to capture the thoughts that flash quickly before us." Christine swept dark brown hair behind her ear.

Audrice stretched her long legs over the matching ottoman.

Christine held up the red *Discover* sign for the camera. "Audrice, would you tell us what you are passionate about that has been a thorn in your side? What do you feel is taking your peace?"

9.1   WHY CAN'T YOU LOVE ME?

"My personal injustice has to do with issues related to male energy. I'm feeling pushed aside and ignored by both a male friend and my son. They don't give me the love and the attention I need. Sometimes they shut me out of their lives—and I feel that is unfair."

Christine nodded.

Audrice continued. "And I find myself getting angry—very angry lately—a lot of hostility comes up. It starts with annoyance, but it sits there and festers and becomes real anger."

A look of concern crossed Christine's face.

"I don't feel like my son loves me as a son should love his mother. I wonder why he doesn't love me—I'm a wonderful soul— but he doesn't seem to see it. I feel alone, I feel . . ." Audrice laughed. "Oh, my brain is going blank!"

Christine smiled at her friend.

"I'm realizing that the real issue is my thought pattern, but I still feel like I can't move past my thinking. So, I ask myself—okay, how is it that you do that to yourself?" Audrice stroked her gray hair.

Christine listened carefully.

"Then I wonder, well, do I love them in the same way? You know, I think I do, but then I come to realize that some of my love is conditional. I'm going to do this so you will love me. I'm going to treat you well so you will love me. See, I treat you so well, why can't you love me?"

Christine stood silently facing the camera.

"Now what I'm trying to do is get to the bigger issue. It's not really about how they are treating me, but it is about how I'm feeling about it," Audrice surmised.

"Yeah," Christine nodded. "Audrice, what is your worst fear surrounding that injustice?"

"That I will be alone," Audrice replied quickly. "That no one will want to be with me."

"That you're not lovable," Christine paraphrased.

"That I'm not lovable, that I'm too strange, . . . that I'm too weird. You know, I do march to a different drummer. And if I'm not accepted, I won't be loved and then I'll be alone—I'll be abandoned." Audrice articulated her angst.

"Were there abandonment issues in your childhood?" Christine probed.

"Oh, yeah," Audrice admitted.

"And how did they manifest?" Christine wondered.

"Uh, well, I always felt close to my father when I was young. I was like his special child because he delivered me. I didn't have the same issues that my sister had, but I had mine. But, one day he totally abandoned us—he just up and left and never came back!" Audrice exclaimed.

"Did you speak with him after that?"

"Nope, I never spoke to him," Audrice divulged.

"Do you know if he's still alive?" Christine asked.

"No, he's dead. He has since deceased."

"Do you feel that you never sent him the love that you wanted to?" Christine questioned.

"It's possible. I feel some emotions coming up right now. When I was in counseling years ago, the counselor kept saying to me 'Well, what about your father?' because I always talked about mother and how I hated her. I hated my mother because she was so mean to me—she was jealous because my father treated me special. And that brings up another issue I have. I've been feeling a lot of jealousy with the anger—I'm jealous when my friend and son pay attention to others instead of me. Do you see the pattern, Christine? It's all a route to something way down here from before," Audrice touched her heart.

9.2   FEELINGS FLOW DEEP

"Perhaps there is a reason why your little soul vibrated into this family where there wasn't enough love to go around. Lack of attention could be a past-life lesson that is even deeper than what you're aware of with your own parents and now you see it manifesting in your friend and son. You really don't want to pass this burden onto the next generation," Christine intuited.

"Right, so how do you change that?" Audrice wondered.

"Good question, Audrice."

"Just now talking to you, I feel like I really am stuck when I speak about my father. Yes, I believe he really abandoned me, and there has never been closure there," Audrice recalled, digging in her purse for a tissue.

"That's right," Christine nodded.

"Never." Audrice's face expressed her sadness.

"And there needs to be closure—even though he's not physically on the planet. We *Discover* that each one—their spirit—does not die. Through the *Peace Process* we'll access the love you have for your father and send it to him so you will have closure on that," Christine promised.

"I'm feeling a lot of emotion about this." Audrice blew her nose.

"Because the truth is, it's not about your current male friend not loving you," Christine said softly.

"You're right, it's all about my father." Tears began to flow. "And how he cared for me."

"It's all about your father, and that . . .." Christine began.

". . . that he went away." Audrice finished.

"He's not here, so you don't know where to send your love. As you know, love doesn't come from your son Brian or your friend Ray. Love is your spiritual essence—and your love comes from you! The heart organ pumps blood—your physical life force, and genes carry the life program of your parents. They divorced and he went away and never came back. Audrice, that is not the story that you want to write for the ending of your life," Christine said gently.

"No, no. I really love my father. I felt special when he was there, because no matter how my mother treated me all week, when he came home on the weekends I felt safe and I felt special and I felt love. My mother never loved me." Audrice shook her head, still holding her tissue.

"But, the 'special' relationship is 'special' love, and that limits your ability to love everyone equally. Special love chooses one over the other and that is hurtful. It was upsetting to your mother that your father rejected her in favor of his daughter," Christine explained.

"Right, right," Audrice agreed.

"So, can you see how it's unkind when you pick just one as being special? We must be equal in God's sight—even equal to his beloved son, which means you are just as treasured." Christine held up the *Discover* sign.

9.3   THE WRONG PERCEPTION OF LOVE

"The first time issues came up about my father was years ago when I attended a seminar. People in the class represented my family—one was my sister, one was my aunt, and there was a young guy that was my son. I was unable to express my anger, and that made everybody in the room mad. Okay, that brought up all this stuff, and I ran under the blackboard and cried hysterically."

Christine listened intently.

"You see, I realized then that my father had this wild sexual relationship with my mother, but he also had been with my sister—yet he never touched me. That was always a big issue for me, yet I sensed it was a mixed bag. I felt loved by him because I was special, but I perceived there was something wrong with me because he never came to my room," Audrice recalled.

"Yeah, and you never understood that he was protecting you."

"I couldn't understand as a child why he never did those things with me—not knowing what those things were. But, I perceived that as love," Audrice said candidly.

"Where are you in the family order of your siblings?" Christine wondered.

"I'm the last one," Audrice answered.

"So, you're the baby," Christine restated. "How many brothers and how many sisters?"

"Just one sister, because the others died and my half-sister wasn't his child. But, he delivered me . . ." Audrice reiterated.

"Yeah," Christine remembered.

". . . at home," Audrice continued.

"Audrice, your father truly loved you and was protecting you, even from his own demons," Christine reassured her friend.

"Yeah, I guess." Audrice sniffed. "But, I still wonder why my father didn't choose me."

"Aw," Christine said gently.

"How come Ray can't love me? How come my own son can't love me? Am I not worthy of that?" Audrice asked.

"Love is not sex, love is not food. Love is eternal and true love never dies," Christine affirmed.

"I guess I have the wrong perception of love," Audrice chuckled, clutching her tissue.

9.4 WHAT IS TRUE LOVE?

"Audrice, countless books have been written from many different perspectives about love. Love is only one thing—and that is everything. Love is the power of the universe that glues your molecules together. God recognizes your spirit and everything that is yours—your mind, your arms, and even your toes! Your spirit goes on and on and on, and that is the love we are looking for. We are searching for the love that transcends the body," Christine reminded her friend.

"I really, truly feel this is another major breakthrough for me. For several weeks now, these issues have come up and I keep saying, oh, I don't like feeling like that—I want to feel better. I want to feel love. I don't want to feel anger, you know, I really want to change—I want to be different," Audrice said sincerely.

"What is true love? Audrice, you will find true love when you *Discover* the power of love alive within yourself. In union with that power you will be connected to your father, because he's just another cell in the larger body that we share."

Audrice nodded.

"You need to let the love flow and that's what we're going to do. Your issue—the thorn in your side—is that your father left home and never returned to resolve your relationship." Christine put the *Discover* placard on the end table.

9.5   LOVED, LOVABLE, AND LOVING

"So, with that, let's go to *Envision*, the creative color orange," Christine said as she picked up the next sign. "We'll take this opportunity to imagine how you want to write the story of your life. Remember the childhood issues you wished to transcend, Audrice? Talk about how you found the positive path by sharing the basic energy of love with everyone. You can describe the story of your life under the headline: *Audrice Collins Is Loved, Lovable, and Loving*," Christine smiled.

"I like that." Audrice beamed.

"Now, you write your story," Christine encouraged.

"I could say that I would like my life to be this and I would like to have that and blah, blah, blah, blah, blah! But, what I'm going to *Envision* today, I think, is deeper. I want to *Envision* myself feeling loved and feeling lovable—knowing, really knowing that I behave lovingly so that love radiates from me. If I could master my vision, then I know my world would change. By being love and not hostility and anger and lack—then my whole world would change."

Christine nodded.

"Yes, I would have a recreational vehicle, a house in Connecticut, and a place here, too—and be able to travel back and forth to see my loving family. A wonderful man would be in my life to appreciate me and share my interests. I realize I can *Envision* those things, but if I'm not coming from a place of love . . ."

"You won't match." Christine shook her head.

"My vision would be for me to become the word 'love' in every area of my life," Audrice concluded.

"You wear it on your forehead." Christine smiled.

"We're going to get to that," Audrice said.

"Here comes love!" Christine laughed heartily.

9.6   MATCH THE VIBRATION OF LOVE

"Yeah, maybe I can change my energy to match my desire instead of holding anger and hostility and creating a negative reality."

"That's right," Christine nodded. "Your goal is, as you say, to be the love you're looking for."

"Yeah. I want to be love because if I'm not, I can desire until doomsday and I might get a little here and there. But, most of it will be the same old shit I got all of my life, because that's what I keep thinking. Once I believe I am worth it and I know that I'm loving—I will be appreciated and loved."

"Everything that you think returns to you because your thoughts are like radio signals," Christine explained.

"Right," Audrice agreed.

"The universe plays back the thoughts you transmit."

"So, my vision would be to change the channel in my brain to one of love which means I would stay focused—like how I brush my teeth. I can brush my teeth with my eyes closed. I know how to brush my teeth—I don't need any instructions! I want my thinking to be like that," Audrice said passionately.

"It's a habit," Christine nodded. "A habit of love."

"Right, a habit of love is what I *Envision* so everything in my life is love." Audrice smiled.

"Perhaps you see that love is not what you thought it was as a child?" Christine grinned.

"No, no, it's not—I see that now. I guess old habits die hard—they just don't want to leave because they're comfortable. But, Christine, I really don't want them anymore. I want the rest of my life in retirement to be happy and joyful and loving," Audrice affirmed.

"We can *Envision* those old habits that you have held for so long to be like my neighbors' house, which recently burned down. In about an hour, their yellow three-story house . . ."

"It was gone." Audrice had seen the charred remains.

". . . was gone," Christine echoed.

"That would be fine with me! An hour would be good." Audrice chuckled.

"We'll burn the old structure down and we will bless the ashes as they fall back upon the earth. Let's ask the world to create a more loving home for our spirit, alright?" Christine asked as she placed the sign labeled *Envision* on top of the stack.

"Okay," Audrice nodded.

9.7   LIVING AS LOVE

Christine picked up the yellow placard labeled *Plan*. "And now, we assign resources like time, and people—perhaps even money to reach our goals and fulfill our dreams."

"The *Plan* for how to be love," Audrice sighed.

"Yes, how to live as love. Audrice, what would be the most loving thing you could do for yourself today?" Christine asked.

"Today? Be here," Audrice said promptly.

"Ah, I think you are already on the right path!" Christine laughed.

"I know I'm supposed to be teaching the *Peace Process*, but somehow I still feel stuck in my own story. As a facilitator, I think it is good to occasionally do the process with someone else," Audrice acknowledged.

"Of course," Christine confirmed.

"I guess my *Plan* is to be more loving and to spend more time on the things that feed my spirit. I've already created the most wonderful job in the world in addition to facilitating the *Peace Process*. I really love my job as an acupuncturist assistant because I'm able to help other people, which is very, very rewarding!" Audrice glowed.

"Your environment supports you," Christine restated.

"Yes, and Jere Proctor, the woman I work with, is an absolutely wonderful soul—a quiet soul, but very blessed."

Christine nodded.

"I've been spending a lot of my income supporting my physical health. Because I created an unloving environment, my body decided that it needed a lot of extra stuff to keep it going. By creating more loving areas in my life that feed my spirit, I *Plan* to choose holistic health care because it's wonderful—and not because I think my body is falling apart," Audrice explained.

"Right," Christine agreed.

"Maybe I'll get to a point where I'll do other joyful things!" Audrice exclaimed.

"What about a walk in the park?" Christine suggested. "Is there a place where you could get in touch with nature?"

"Oh, yeah. The beach would be a very good environment. I don't walk on the beach, but I found a place where I can walk and still see the water."

"What about sunrise or sunset—could you go to a place at dawn or dusk to boost your energy?" Christine wondered.

"Sunsets are nice—I'm not usually awake at sunrise," Audrice replied.

"Audrice, is there a bench where you could sit and watch the sunset every day?" Christine asked.

"Yes—I live in a beautiful place. I haven't enjoyed it as much because I've created an environment where I don't have anyone to share it with," Audrice observed.

"Mmm." Christine nodded.

"This week I asked my neighbors to go for a walk with me. The next night, they asked me to walk with them to see the sunset. And I felt better when I came home—I felt more like me."

Christine smiled at her friend.

Audrice continued. "I've been working on a *Plan* to choose not to be around people with negative energy. As I get more in touch with my feelings, I'll know when someone doesn't support me in being loving, and I'll choose not to be around that person. But, I'll do it lovingly instead of being angry and hostile."

"It is not anyone's fault that you're not feeling love, Audrice. Can you bless people where they are?"

"Sure. I can bless them for bringing me what I don't want, as I become clearer that I want to feel love—and not those negative emotions."

"Yes, you can recognize the calls for love, which are anger, fear, and worry—because people with negative energy need love," Christine affirmed.

"Right, and turn around and be able to send them love," Audrice added. "And that would be the *Plan* for learning to love myself—practicing my Qi Gong, meditating, and getting a little more organized."

"Your environment reflects your state of mind—a cluttered environment shows that you are thinking about too much stuff," Christine observed.

"I do! I have too much stuff and I keep trying to get rid of it. But, stuff comes back again and I don't know why." Audrice laughed.

"Ask yourself if somebody else could use what you have. You don't have to hold onto anything, because there is enough to go around. Open your hands and let the energy flow," Christine suggested.

"All my life I've bought things in consignment shops. This week, I went out and bought two new handbags—I just felt that I deserved something brand-new. When I came home, I got rid of some old stuff."

"Hmm," Christine nodded. "Audrice, what about a gratitude journal?"

"Yeah, I did that every day for a long time, and it really helped. In the morning, I got up and thanked God for being there and I wrote thoughts of appreciation on my gratitude list. If I didn't write in the morning, I would write at night before I went to bed," Audrice explained.

"Is your mother still alive?" Christine wondered.

"No." Audrice shook her head. "She died."

"Perhaps the *Plan* will have to include your parents, because they provided the perfect environment for your spirit to grow. You inherited patterns of jealousy and abandonment that you need to heal," Christine surmised.

"Right," Audrice agreed.

"They were your perfect parents," Christine added.

"But, I never was a perfect daughter!" Audrice laughed.

"Perfect is always *what is*. We don't know what it's all about—we're not supposed to—because it's much larger than what we can see."

"Suddenly, I feel like I got lost in the love and what I really want because I know that includes my father. So, the *Plan* would have to include releasing my emotion," Audrice reasoned.

"That's right," Christine agreed.

"The *Plan* might be to find a way to send him love even though he's passed over."

"And your mother . . ." Christine interjected.

"Yeah, my meditation has to send love to both of them," Audrice realized.

"That's what we'll do," Christine concurred.

"Maybe a *Plan* would be to work on sending my father love because I felt like I did have closure with my mother. You see, she had lost her mind and for two years when I was with her she never knew me. Then one day, she said, 'Audrey.' And she knew who I was! I went over and she said, 'I'm so sorry.' She said, 'I never meant to hurt you. I'm so sorry if I didn't give you enough love.' The tears just overwhelmed me, because I had been in spiritual counseling, and the minister said that it was God's grace to hear those words from my mother's mouth."

"Right." Christine nodded.

"After all these years, I always thought my father loved me and my mother didn't. But, I've come to terms with her—I don't hate her anymore," Audrice confided.

"Because, she did love you." Christine tapped her heart.

"She did, in the only way that she could—she didn't know how to love any other way," Audrice confirmed.

"And, she set you up to heal—she showed you how withholding love is hurtful. Now, it's your time to make amends."

"Alright, am I done with the *Plan* or am I still planning?" Audrice asked.

"I think that the only way to heal your injustice is to send both parents love because they gave you a body and you were their perfect daughter," Christine concluded.

"So, let me recap. In order for me to be love, which is what I want to do to change my life, my *Plan* is to do as many loving things as I can for me—feed myself love, send my parents love, and really come to closure with my father," Audrice summarized.

"And since they're not here, it's going to be true love because you're not going to expect anything back," Christine pointed out.

"Right, right—because they can't return it. They can't pay attention to me like Ray or my son because they're not here," Audrice reasoned.

"But, guess what? The miracle of love is that you can send it right where you are because we all exist in the same body of God.

169

Through God's grace, you will know that you are part of the eternal love that is divine," Christine explained.

"Okay." Audrice nodded. "It really is about feeling the love. Somehow, feeling more love for me."

"Love will come back after you send it out—but, you don't control when and you don't control how your love is returned. So, we are going to find true love—unconditional love. I think we've got the right *Plan* because love is what flows from you naturally." Christine put the yellow placard labeled *Plan* on the stack of signs.

9.8 THE SECRET OF LOVE

"So, to experience love I treat myself more lovingly and do more loving things?" Audrice questioned.

"The *Work* is to send love from your heart to what's taking your peace. As you experience your love in meditation, you will know that you are loving." Christine held up the green sign for the *Work* discipline. "So, Audrice, get comfortable for our meditation and place both feet on the floor."

"Okay." Audrice planted her feet.

"Now, close your eyes . . . take a deep breath, inhale fully and then let it out . . . *ahh*. Let's do that again. Inhale from below your belly button, fill your lungs like two party balloons and let me hear you say . . ."

"*Ahh* . . ." Audrice let go of her tension.

"Let's take another deep breath. Inhale, this time from your toes. Lift your shoulders with as much air as you can take in and let it all out. *Ahh* . . . settle down . . . relax." Christine paused.

"The lilies in the field do not strain to be themselves," Christine quoted the gospel of Matthew, "and neither should you. You are lovable, you are loving, and you are loved. You are a child of God and you can't change that—no matter what you do. It's not about being good or bad because God has never judged you. He loves you always and forever—just as you are," Christine said slowly.

Audrice shifted in the chair.

"Be the child of God that simply extends the love you've been given. See, love in action comes from your loving thoughts. You think to take a step forward, and then you begin to walk. In this same way, put the desire in your heart to send your father love. Then, call to him and send the innocent love of a child for a parent. Your father's spirit needs your love. He walked out the door never to return—yet he is somewhere within the universe."

Christine continued. "Let us ask God to deliver this message to your father. Know that you can still love even when death seems to have shut the door. You can send love always—no matter what, because death does not hinder true love."

Audrice sat quietly, her face serene.

"Sometimes, the body just gets in the way—we think that by giving a kiss we are loving. Yet, Judas showed betrayal by kissing

Jesus. So, a kiss is not love, but it could be—as anything done with the right intent is loving," Christine reassured.

"Audrice, I want you to do everything in your life with love. When you get up, be grateful. When you walk down the street, smile at a stranger—send your love, because love is meant to be shared. The irony is that love is returned when it's given away."

Audrice breathed softly.

"Those you perceive love you, as I do, are simply feeling their own love—and joyously so, because they give freely from their heart. So, you see, the secret of love is that in the instant you give your love, you receive the love of God from deep within yourself," Christine reflected.

"Now, let us send your mother that same love. She did love you by being the thorn that provoked within you intense passion, jealousy, and anger! But, the resentment you felt for her points two fingers back at yourself. Because, you know, if you feel negative emotions, they must be within you—and only you can release them. Your mother withheld her love from you—so that you could find love within yourself."

Audrice shifted again in the chair.

"When you feel love you will know what love truly is. Love is not a special relationship. Love is not conditional. Love is freely given, equally for all. Let your environment support you in being loving. Give the trees a hug—they deserve to be loved, too, for they support you and give you oxygen. See how animals show up to remind you that they are your friends in nature. We are one family on one planet in a very, very large universe!"

Christine continued. "Forgive yourself for needing the lesson—polish the windows of your soul and let your light shine. Feel the love of God through you and you will know where home is. When you shed your body, you will find your way, because you are light and you are energy. You don't need to accept this truth from me—someday you will recognize it yourself. God loves you and I love you—feel that love. Thanks be to God, and with that we say *Amen*," Christine concluded.

"Audrice, when you're ready, you can open your eyes."

Audrice took a deep breath.

"We know our *Work* is done, because thought sets everything else in motion."

"You make it sound so simple," Audrice laughed.

"Love is simple." Christine set the green placard down on the stack of warm-colored signs. "Love is simple!"

9.9   YES, WE CAN!

"Okay, Audrice—now, let's *Measure*." Christine picked up the blue sign. "How did you do? Did you feel the love that you were looking for?"

"The meditation was nice—I have a lot of insight as to how to create the love I want in my life. I'd like to just blink my eyes and make it happen! Hmm . . . I have no trouble thinking about what I don't want—I just wish I could press a button and turn my brain off." Audrice chuckled.

Christine smiled at her friend.

"The *Work* would be really sticking to my *Plan* of gratitude and seeing people with more love and not falling back into my old patterns. By doing more loving things, I feel that I can change!" Audrice declared.

"Audrice, you don't need to try too hard to be what you already are. The only thing you need to do is bless the old pattern, because that will change your negative thoughts into positive ones," Christine suggested.

"Mm-hmm. Well, yeah, part of me knows I can't be what others expect me to be. I need to be me and if people want to be with me, then fine—but, if they don't, that has to be okay, too," Audrice realized.

"Right," Christine agreed. "The false belief is that others don't give you what you deserve. Since you're responsible for your thoughts, you have the power to feel love. Audrice, I think you understand what love is now."

"I'm getting a better idea of what love is, yeah. You know, I always said, a true sign of love is when people do loving things for you and don't expect anything in return," Audrice affirmed.

"Just like you sent love to your parents in the meditation without expecting anything in return. You know, I was thinking, Audrice—your father's leaving the family triggered your emotional reaction."

"Mm-hmm." Audrice nodded.

"So, you must have carried the pattern of abandonment in your soul, and that impression is very deep. If you can heal that . . ." Christine began.

"Would I be healing just in this life or the past?" Audrice wondered.

"If you heal your past now," Christine believed, "you don't have to pass the same pattern onto your children."

"I already did!" Audrice laughed. "You know, one of my final issues is to really find me. And, I think that's going to be allowing my love out because my potential to love is already there."

"It's already there," Christine echoed.

"I'm the one who stops it," Audrice recognized. "That's really what I want—to let my love flow. I'm being honest, you know."

"Yes, I can see that." Christine nodded.

"It's still a big step for me. I think I have accomplished a lot. I'd like to say, now I am love and I will be for the rest of my life— but, I'm not really truly feeling that yet," Audrice admitted.

"You can set the intention and make the commitment," Christine told her.

"Right," Audrice affirmed.

"And then check yourself on your commitment," Christine added.

"Yeah, I think that's about where I'm at. I run this process in my mind and sometimes I don't *Measure* as well as I'd like to. But, the more I use it the more I'm going to learn. I realize I'm still learning, because I'm seeing things differently. I guess that's what *Measure* is really all about—seeing differently," Audrice surmised.

"That's right, because you *Measure* from your direct experience," Christine said as she put the sign down. "First, you have an experience and then you ask yourself—well, how did that experience make me feel?"

Audrice nodded.

9.10   CREATE LOVING SITUATIONS

"The final discipline is to *Value* your *Peace Process* session." Christine picked up the indigo-colored sign.

"The *Value* of the whole process would be that I am able to vibrate to love like I *Envision* by creating the *Plan* and loving the *Work* of becoming love. Then, I'm going to *Measure* much better. I will not let unloving people push my buttons. I will be loving, whether or not they are attentive to me. I'll offer my loving energy to those who need love," Audrice concluded.

"You'll recognize the calls for love?" Christine asked.

"Yes, and I won't put a price tag on it."

"Love is priceless," Christine agreed.

"You're right, the *Value* of being love is that I'm going to create more loving situations. My life is going to be happier and more joyful. My body is going to respond to that love, too. I won't have a pain in my shoulder, a heel spur, or an allergy . . ."

"Or a toe cramp." Christine grinned.

"I felt like my body was falling apart this year—but, I see now that my spirit wants to emerge and my body has been distracting me."

"Mmm, you must take a firm stand for your spirit—and to those distractions say no!" Christine exclaimed.

"I've made up my mind, and I am not allowing this negative energy. My spiritual self has to emerge totally. And, I really believe when my spirit takes over, there will be no room for negativity."

"That's right," Christine agreed.

"So, that was a good insight, and that came out even though I felt like I didn't *Measure* too well!" Audrice laughed. "I'm just being truthful. I could sit here and say, oh yeah—blah, blah, blah, blah, blah."

"And, your honesty is an important aspect of *Measure*," Christine replied.

"The other *Value* I see is that I picked basically one subject today but I have other issues, like selling my house and the fact that I don't want to be alone—but, those are all connected," Audrice reasoned.

"Right." Christine nodded.

"The fact that my house is not selling is just one more manifestation of my not loving myself enough," Audrice recognized.

"Yes," Christine confirmed.

"I think—oh, I should move back there, because I can't sell it—blah, blah. All negative stuff because I'm not feeling loved. I wonder who's going to put up with me? It's all connected—all part of the same pattern." Audrice smiled. "Anyway, I thank you."

"I value your friendship, Audrice, and your willingness to go through the *Peace Process* because you contribute to world peace by giving up a little corner of your own conflict. And, I thank you." Christine smiled as she placed the *Value* placard on the stack of rainbow-colored signs.

"Did we do our time limit?" Audrice asked.

Christine checked the video monitor. "We did."

"Exactly, too!" Audrice was amazed.

"We did very well," Christine nodded.

Audrice stood up. "Oh man, look at that—right on time!"

"I love you." Christine threw her arms around Audrice.

"It will be interesting to see how much love pours out." Audrice bent down to embrace Christine.

"That's right," Christine agreed.

"It isn't that I can't be loving, but I want afterwards to feel, to really feel loving—and not care how people respond," Audrice realized.

"Right, we need to consider what motivates our actions," Christine acknowledged.

"Yeah, am I doing loving things because I expect a response or am I loving because that's what I am," Audrice mused.

Christine opened her arms and spread her fingers wide. "Audrice, love asks for nothing."

9.11   EXERCISE

1.   Can you identify any unresolved childhood issues?

2.   Sometimes we move our old dramas to a new stage with different characters. Describe your issues that reflect a pattern in your life.

3.   List the ways you might change old negative thought patterns to new habits of love.

10

My Peaceful Purpose

Let there be peace on Earth, and let it begin with me.

—Jill Jackson & Sy Miller

Kim Fisichella stood at the checkout counter in the health food store and while she waited, a colorful flyer caught her attention: *Spiritual Adventure in Costa Rica.* Kim picked up the flyer and read with interest: *Destiny calls eleven women to learn the Peace Process in paradise. We will walk in the rain forest, relax in the hot springs, and view the active Arenal Volcano on 64 acres of sacred land. Surrounded by organic orchards in a private sanctuary that overlooks the largest lake in Costa Rica, you will be transformed with gentle yoga, meditation, and dream journal.*

    Kim went home and shared the information with Tony, her husband. "Honey, the cost of the trip includes meals, activities, classes, and excursions to the Hanging Bridges, Arenal Volcano, Tabacon Hot Springs, Rio Fortuna Waterfall, and the Danaus Eco-Center. It's the week of March 11–18. What do you think?"

"You know, Kim, I've heard that peace is the national treasure in Costa Rica. I think this White Eagle Retreat Center might help calm your nerves," Tony approved.

"It says here we'll learn about the natural history of butterflies in Costa Rica, like blue morpho, monarch, and swallowtail. You know, I'm such a nature lover—just imagine walking in an orchard with 1,000 pineapples!"

"I can take the girls to school and look after your parents. Why don't you go?" Tony asked.

"Oh, I was hoping you would say that. Mom's dementia has really affected my moods lately. This retreat seems like the answer to my prayers!" She gave her husband a big hug.

Kim picked up the flyer again to read Christine's brief biography. *Christine's vision of the peace symbol at the beach in the year 2000 inspired her to write more than 57 inches of material in 19 binders known as The Christine Revelation. She is writing a trilogy of sacred texts and publishing the good news. Christine is birthing awareness of the feminine Christ on this women's retreat in Costa Rica.*

Kim thought about how understanding Tony had just been. Never had she asked for personal time away from the family. But, she knew she was broken—there was only so much more she could take. Kim hesitated for a moment, and then she picked up the telephone to call Christine and reserve her place in paradise.

10.1 *PEACE PROCESS* IN PARADISE

Kim sat in a rocking chair on the outdoor patio at the White Eagle Retreat Center. Christine faced her, ready to begin the *Peace Process*. "Kim, what takes your peace?" Christine asked.

"I'm so busy with everybody else and their problems, there is no time to take care of me. I needed to get away so that I could find some peace of mind and find out what my life is all about—what my purpose is." Kim rocked in the cool Costa Rican air.

"Mmm, so it's just a little bit of soul searching and taking a breath and stepping back to let you see how busy you've been," Christine restated.

"And, how stressed." Kim added.

"And, the stress of the world," Christine echoed. "What causes you the most stress? Where does your stress come from?" Christine probed.

"Probably, mostly fighting at the house. The boys in my house—my husband and my stepson—are Italian and they have very strong tempers." Kim smiled. "I mean—their expression is strong—and very loud. Between them and the twins, we have noise pollution in our house all the time. It's always so noisy and that creates a lot of stress for me."

"Kim, where do you see yourself spending most of your time and energy? Where does your energy go?" Christine wondered.

"Health care, child care, and parent care—I spend all of my time either assisting my children, my husband, my parents, or keeping the house clean and cooking." Kim flashed a big smile.

"So, you're at that age where you are in the middle of both children and parents with a husband. Which could mean you have help available—but it seems that you are in service to those relationships. As well, you are doing all the cooking and cleaning," Christine reiterated.

"And, trying to work on my Masters' degree right now," Kim added.

"And school! Ah, well. There is no doubt that you need a vacation. It's easy to see where your stress is coming from. There are just so many hours in the day and they're all used up—with none left over for you to rejuvenate and regenerate," Christine empathized.

Kim rocked slowly.

"So, that's what we're here to do with the *Peace Process*—to *Discover* the source of your stress and bring you back into balance. We want to connect to the source of life and take the time to fill up your tank so that your vehicle will continue to run and not be left on the side of the road," Christine explained.

Kim nodded.

"Now, what happens if you don't find your balance?" Christine asked plainly.

"I will add to the stress quite a bit. I will add to the negativity at some point. And, none of us will be healthy in mind, body, or spirit. So, as the mother and daughter and wife, I want to be the one that adds the positive energy—and the smiles in my family," Kim said candidly, wisps of her blonde hair blowing across her face.

"And, besides your other roles, you're taking on another one at school. What is that?" Christine inquired.

"I'm learning ways to heal people through natural methods like homeopathy and herbology—methods that have been around for 5,000 years. Hopefully, I can teach others to live with better health." Kim responded.

"Kim, what's the worst that could happen if you can't balance?" Christine asked frankly.

"We'll have a dysfunctional family. I don't want the children to grow up with stress and have a lot of struggle in their lives. I'd like to teach them how to find their inner peace and be happy with positive energy." Kim's warm brown eyes sparkled.

"So, you want to be a positive role model for your children. That sounds like an opportunity then—and perhaps motivation for you to take this positive path. Kim, let's talk about what you think the benefits will be if you choose to balance this equation. What is the up side of all this?" Christine questioned.

"Well, a lot of positive energy, which I believe will be spread much further than our household. Both my parents are in poor health and I think they will benefit, because the stress they feel at our house affects their health quite a bit. And, I hope that my twin daughters will go out into the world and model health and positive energy. Part of alternative health is also teaching—not just the body, but the mind and the spirit. You have to come from all angles to become healthy and whole." Kim smiled.

"Absolutely," Christine agreed. "And, what will you do with your degree?"

"Um, I'll probably be a counselor—I still need fourteen courses. It will take me about a year to get through each course at this point because I just don't have time for that." Kim shrugged her shoulders.

"So, your courses will create career opportunities for you," Christine restated.

"Yes," Kim nodded. "I'll be a teacher at some point—or work with somebody—I could possibly work with a doctor."

"Mm-hmm. And, as you work you could get help with the house cleaning, perhaps?" Christine suggested.

"If I have the money to pay for a house keeper that would be very helpful!" Kim laughed.

"And, let other people do the things that are not really in your heart to do," Christine recommended.

"Absolutely," Kim approved.

"Or, at least you've done it enough where, you know, you wouldn't mind sharing now," Christine clarified.

"Oh, I don't mind at all!" Kim shook her head.

"So, we'd like to ask the universe for some help in that department." Christine grinned.

"That's not the department where I want to excel. I would like to excel at the healing part," Kim chuckled.

"Right, you have a natural ability and an opportunity to use your talents. Some of the stress that you're feeling is your soul steering you in this direction. So, there's a lot of motivation for taking the healing path," Christine explained.

"Absolutely," Kim agreed.

"From what I have heard you say, you are here to *Discover* why you've come to Costa Rica and to learn how to balance mind, body, and spirit. And, I am watching that happen this week. I've seen you smile as you walk," Christine observed.

"Oh, I love the nature here—it's so beautiful." Behind Kim, a crow called loudly—*caw, caw, caw!*

"I've seen your tranquil face in yoga as you learn to stay balanced in the postures—and feel good afterwards."

Kim nodded.

"And, I've seen you wanting to call home to your family. Never really forgetting about them, but knowing that a better you makes your family better, right?" Christine surmised.

"You are absolutely right about that," Kim confirmed.

10.2   BALANCED IN MIND, BODY, AND SPIRIT

"You are very motivated to be centered and at peace with your spirit. As we *Discover* all of the ways your energy is taken, we can imagine how to set boundaries that honor each of your relationships. Your true role is a function of love for all with enough time for yourself and for your family," Christine concluded.

Kim nodded as she rocked.

"Well, Kim, let's *Envision* what it will look like if the cover of *"O" Magazine* read: *Balanced in Mind, Body, and Spirit. How to go from stressed out to peaceful.* Now, wouldn't everyone want to know how you do it?"

With a big smile, Kim brushed back her blonde bangs.

"And, the entire feature article is about you at peace in your tranquil home. How did you turn a stressful environment into a peaceful place? Everybody wants to know! So, tell me what the article says. How did you do it?" Christine sat back in her chair.

"First, I want to say, thank you, Christine. You've been a very big influence. I have been searching for a very long time. And, I've had some excellent teachers along the way. But, where I'm at now is by far the furthest I've come and the best I've felt in a very long time." Kim smiled. "So, I guess realizing that I am responsible—and no one else—for finding balance in life in order to share positive energy."

Christine listened carefully.

Kim continued. "And, it will be necessary for me to lovingly and gently tell others what I want. It has been very difficult for me to tell people when they're influencing my life in a negative way. Christine, remember when you described a candle with the wick being the core strength in the middle? Well, the wick of my candle needs to be stronger to support the flame of my passion. To have my spirit glow, I need to correct that."

"You want to speak your truth and be strong in your center. So, setting boundaries is an absolute must for your spirit," Christine reflected.

"Yes that's it, and I want to be clear about my purpose. I really have to dig deep and find out why I am here. What are my lessons to learn? I would venture to say most people couldn't answer that question. So, this retreat is helping me find the answers I need," Kim affirmed.

"And, have you found your purpose?" Christine asked.

"I believe so," Kim answered honestly.

"Can you share that with us?"

"I believe my purpose in life this time is to be a healer. Actually, it's funny because most of my healing has been focused on the body—but it's the mind and spirit also. And, I believe that all three have to be balanced. I believe my purpose is to learn more about how to do that and how to help others. So, my purpose is mostly to help others, the world, and myself. Reach out and touch them and teach them how they also can have peace. And, with peace and love, there would be no stress, no conflicts—and no war!" Kim exclaimed.

"What will you do, what do you see yourself doing, as you go back to that environment that needs adjustment? What does the article say that you did? How did you make the necessary change at home?" Christine probed.

"The first thing I'm going to do is write down several quotes that meant a lot to me. Something simple, like what you said—

you're perfect just the way you are. I am perfect just the way I am. I'm going to work with my eight-year-olds and have them help me make little signs that I can put up around the house. They will remind everybody how we need to live."

Christine listened quietly.

Kim continued. "To find ourselves, we need to accept each other as we are. So, I've got some wonderful quotes for inspiration—and then I need to set my boundaries. I need to find time to meditate every day and to work on my purpose. Also, it is important to free everyone else to be responsible. So, I must choose when to be a caregiver and when to step back."

"Beautiful! Well, I love your dream. Just a few small changes will make a big difference for you, your children, and the family as you model balanced mind, body, and spirit. I'm sure that will motivate other women who dearly love their husbands, children, and their parents. If you find a way to bring the balance back within yourself and let others have the responsibility for their own lives, then you can truly be their teacher by modeling what you believe," Christine summarized.

"I've decided that I'm going to get rid of the TV for myself. I've been a fanatic a little bit with the news—that's probably the only television that I watch, but it is very negative. My husband wants to watch movies that are violent, and I've always been a partner with that—but I don't need to be. We can have funny movies and light movies and things that put a smile on your face. Absolutely, that will be the way I will make my life peaceful, and my younger children will learn to do the same. Nobody needs violence," Kim concluded.

"Well, you can use the ear plugs the airlines gave you!" Christine chimed in.

Kim laughed.

"You'll have some good books to read and also some nice positive audio messages. There's no need to change anybody else and their tastes, because you'll have positive things you can substitute," Christine encouraged.

Kim nodded as the breeze blew across the lake.

10.3   AN INSPIRATIONAL MESSAGE

"Now, we're going to *Plan* and schedule activities to help you balance each day. Is there a time that you can reserve for your own meditation, yoga, and listening practice? As you said, you drive the girls to school. Describe how that's going to change. What time of the day is going to be for you? Schedule an appointment with yourself to balance mind, body, and spirit," Christine suggested.

"Okay. First thing in the morning, I have a half-hour drive to drop my girls off at school. On the way home, I will listen to an inspirational message in the car. I'll do the same thing when I go to pick them up. Hopefully, the traffic will cooperate so I can relax and enjoy that." Kim chuckled.

Christine grinned as she gazed at the panorama behind Kim—the gardens, the lake, the mountains—and not a car in sight.

Kim continued. "My husband goes to school every night, and he doesn't come home till ten o'clock. It will be a challenge, but I might try to change things around so I can try to finish everything up by nine o'clock at night—and make that hour mine."

"And, is there any time you can squeeze in the morning maybe just for a little stretch or something to center?" Christine wondered.

"I think so." Kim removed her button-down sweater and draped it over the arm of the rocker.

"Maybe a thought card in the morning to start your day and a thought card at night before you go to sleep?"

"That would be nice," Kim nodded.

"Something simple, it doesn't have to take a lot of time," Christine reminded her.

"Yeah, I'd like to put on the yoga video in the morning when I get a chance as often as I can," Kim agreed.

"Even five minutes to begin breathing would be a wonderful *Plan* and if you had fifteen, even better. But, to try to carve out an hour might not happen for you. If you can think five minutes here, five minutes there, and really make use of the five minutes—that would be a practical *Plan*," Christine suggested.

"Right," Kim confirmed.

"Meditation could begin with five minutes—that's enough. But, gradually you might go ten minutes because it feels good."

"It feels wonderful," Kim smiled.

"As you energize the core of your being with love, more harmony will come to you. And, in the *Peace Process*, the *Plan* is always for peace," Christine concluded.

10.4   PEACE IS WITHIN

"Now, for your *Work*, I'm going to invite you on a guided meditation. We'll send love to the *Plan* for balancing your mind, body, and spirit. Let's include love for your parents, husband, children, and your classes at school. You can even send love to the people that you haven't healed yet but, you are committed to healing by first healing yourself," Christine began.

"All right," Kim allowed.

"So, close your eyes and place both your feet flat on the tile." Christine paused. "Just take a deep breath and relax."

Kim planted her feet and stopped rocking.

"Kim, your *Work* is to send the thought of love to all things and then whatever life brings you—whether it's a telemarketer or a neighbor—you meet that one with kindness, patience, and respect. Let the love radiate from your heart, and strengthen your heart. Utilize the energy of love to turn on your heart like a flashlight. Expand this beam until it becomes a spotlight, searching for all souls in pain and suffering. You recognize the calls for love—anger, fear, and worry—and you will answer."

Kim breathed deeply.

"The healer's journey is a path through trials so you have empathy for others with the same challenges. You are a master healer already, Kim—but you needed to go to the depths of stress and imbalance to find your compassion. People will be comforted by your presence and touched by your soft heart."

A crow broke the silence—*caw, caw, caw*!

Christine continued. "Send out your love to the news and to all the people who create the news. They live in a fearful world and you are the balm that will heal them, the salve for their eyes to help them see that peace is within. Peace is your core being and it stands tall and unwavering like the wick in a candle. The wind blows the flame to and fro, but the wick stands tall. So, you'll have to stand up for what you believe."

Kim sat in the stillness.

"Feel the love for your husband now. He is different from you—that's why you are attracted to him as your opposite. Just meet him with love. Bless his upbringing, so different from yours, and know that there are many lessons to be learned in being with him without giving up who you are," Christine encouraged.

Behind Kim, a hummingbird flew by.

"And, bless your children always—allow them to make mistakes and give them responsibility appropriate for their age. Know that God is their parent, so there is little for you to do but to love them and to let them know that you love them just as they are. We need do nothing to prove our worth and to prove our value. So, we thank God for our existence and we ask that our lives may be a blessing that we extend to others," Christine said slowly.

In the chair, Kim rested quietly.

"The way love is shown here on earth is forgiveness. Not for others, but because you needed the lesson—you wanted to be a healer. You wanted to remember what it felt like to need healing and so you walked that path. Send love then to yourself. Send forgiveness—extend it to others and know that it is yours. And there love is and love has never left you," Christine paused.

Kim breathed softly.

"Be strong in the spiritual ideal of peace, love, and wisdom. Listen to nature; listen to your dreams. Remember this place in your mind and go there as often as you need to." Christine's voice quivered. "Remember the joy and the connection that you felt and the guidance will come and you will know what to do. As you heal, you bless the world and the universe. God and all the angels above watch over you and thank you for sending your love and extending peace into the world that needs it so. Amen."

10.5   DID YOU FEEL THE LOVE?

"So, when you're ready, you can open your eyes."

Kim blinked.

"Now, we'll *Measure* the truth of how you felt you received the meditation and how much love you sent. Did you resist sending love to any situation?" Christine questioned.

"I felt love with everything. There was no resistance, which is exactly how it should be and what I want for myself. I don't think I've met anyone I didn't like, so it's easy in that respect to love everybody. It was just a very peaceful meditation with beautiful words—really heartfelt," Kim said softly.

"And Kim, you can listen to our conversation over and over again. It can be your station, your channel as you remind yourself to strengthen your heart. And, if there is any resistance to sending love as things come up, you can modify the *Plan*. There is a feedback loop. You can go back and ask yourself what would be the *Plan* for harmony in this situation?"

"Yes, that's true. It's very easy here to do it that way. But, when you're in a situation for a while and there's a lot of stress, it's going to be a lot harder to stop yourself and replay—and feel the love—and send the love. I've spent a long time in my life not doing that. Now, I need to learn how to do that again," Kim nodded.

10.6   BREATHE STRESS AWAY

"Right," Christine agreed. "We can learn a breathing technique that might help you. You count sixteen breaths on one hand, using your non-dominant hand as a counter. You can try this now. We can go back into the meditation. Say you are feeling a little stressed, so you go to your quiet place and then you begin to breathe sixteen times. Here we go—put your thumbnail to the nail on your index finger.

And, you can watch me and when you're comfortable, you can close your eyes."

Kim's eyelids lowered.

"Take a nice deep breath. Breathe from your belly button. Let it lift your spine a little straighter and make you taller. As you exhale, slowly and gently bring those shoulders down away from your neck."

Kim sat up and took a deep breath.

"Move your thumb to the first pad and breathe again. Inhale, breathe in to expand your chest and fill your lungs like party balloons. As you exhale, know that the sun is shining gently and equally down upon all, including you."

In the rocking chair, Kim sat quietly.

"Move your thumb to the middle pad and take another breath. Maybe your belly feels extended and the shoulders come up to your ears. But, take it all in—and as you exhale, slowly reverse the process, allowing your shoulders to come down away from your neck."

Kim relaxed into the rhythm of her breath.

"Your thumb moves to the last pad of the index finger and you breathe in. Take in all the oxygen through your nose—you're filtering the air. Lifting up, you breathe in life-force energy. As you exhale, you want to expel all the carbon dioxide out through your nose, taking time to assimilate the oxygen."

Kim nodded, her eyes still closed.

"Your thumb moves to the middle finger, nail to nail. On the inhale, think *I accept* and as you exhale, *the peace of God.* Your thumb moves to the first pad. Inhale, *I accept* and exhale, *the peace of God.* Middle pad, breathe in *I accept.* Exhale, *the peace of God.* So, you become the peace of God. Move your thumb to the last pad. Inhale, *I accept.* As you accept God's life force—which is peace and love—you become peaceful and loved."

As she exhaled, Kim smiled serenely.

"Let's move to the ring finger now, nail to nail. Breathe in, *I accept.* You're accepting your next breath, which means you have something more to do. As you exhale, you know that your function on earth must be to love and forgive yourself."

Kim shifted in the chair.

"Now, move your thumb to the first pad. Inhale, *I accept.* You're going to take on a new role in life and make a commitment—a vow—to God. And, as you exhale, *the peace of God*, you extend more of God's love. How wonderful!" Christine exclaimed.

Kim beamed.

"With a smile on your face, you move your thumb to the middle pad. Inhale. You are starting to feel one with God—one with your source energy. Take it all in. It surrounds you. It's within you, it's outside of you, and it's everywhere. You exhale. That's all you need to do."

Christine continued. "Move your thumb to the last pad as you breathe in, lifting up and surrounding yourself with God's hug for you in this now moment. Exhale, and move your thumbnail to your pinky. Inhale, breathe in. This one is for you. You're going to go out with love as you exhale. That's all you are, that's all you do, you are in heaven now, and you claim it for yourself."

Kim nodded.

"Now, move your thumb to the first pad. Inhale, and breathe in. God loves you, the angels love you, and you are one with them. As you exhale, send out love—magnetizing to yourself all that is good and beautiful, holy and helpful."

Kim's face shone in the morning light.

"Move your thumb to the middle pad. Breathe in deeply, draw the breath in from your toes—draw it from the center of the earth. Let it fill your very being. You can't contain the love anymore! As you expand your love, your energy field grows. Now, exhale slowly."

Christine continued. "On the last pad, inhale and slowly count one, two, three, four, five, six. We're not trying to go to sleep and we're not trying to wake up. We're just going for a nice, balanced breath. Now, exhale one, two, three, four, five, six. And, Kim, when you're ready, you can open your eyes."

10.7 SHARE YOUR PEACE

"So, you can *Measure* how peaceful you feel after sixteen breaths. When you're not centered in love, stop and do those sixteen breaths. Then you will meet the situation with love and peace."

"That makes sense," Kim nodded.

"Now, let's talk about the *Value* of the process and any progress that you have made in our time together."

Kim was thoughtful. "It always helps to have someone to share with because there's feedback. I think when you practice by yourself it often stays within. Another person can help to complete the circle, and offer ideas that haven't occurred to you," Kim observed.

"It might be useful to have a continuing partner to share with once a week—or maybe a group that meets once a month," Christine suggested.

"Right," Kim nodded.

"And even just a short ten-minute phone conversation, with five minutes for each of you could be helpful. You might talk about how you are doing with respect to your goals."

"Good idea, Christine. That would remind me to care for other people. I think inner peace comes from sharing with others, don't you?" Kim asked.

"Yes. Someone who knows the process will know if you're getting stuck somewhere," Christine confirmed.

"Absolutely," Kim agreed.

"You can remind each other to try the sixteen breaths. And, if one of you forgets—well, then you try again next time." Christine grinned.

"Exactly," Kim concurred.

"And, when you have a success, your partner has a success as a result of being helpful. It will help both of you to stay the path," Christine affirmed.

"Definitely. And, if you don't have someone to share with, like so many other things, after awhile the energy goes away." Kim rocked gently.

"An important principle of the *Peace Process* is that you have to give peace in order to get it. We give love and that's what we feel—the feeling of love becomes a memory that lives in our energy field. We allow love to come through us by not blocking it," Christine explained.

"There are so many things in this world that can pull you away from your purpose," Kim declared.

"The video we've made will be a reminder for you to go back and watch yourself making a commitment to your vision of living with love. If you find yourself in an unloving situation, excuse yourself, go back through your feedback loop—and center yourself with sixteen breaths."

"Right." Kim smiled.

"Can you see yourself going to your quiet place with your beautiful essential oils, and maybe your eye pillow? Just a few minutes are all that you really need to trigger yourself back—to remember your purpose."

"Absolutely," Kim nodded.

10.8   A LEGACY OF LOVE

"Kim, can you share any wisdom about how we could use the *Peace Process* on a more expanded scale? Any thoughts about how to do that?" Christine asked.

"I think it would be wonderful to bring the *Peace Process* to groups of high school and elementary students. It could help them find their purpose and learn to siphon out the things they don't need. A few schools might be willing to let someone come in and teach it. Perhaps that school will talk to another school and recommend the process. I really think that starting at a young age would be beneficial. And, hopefully, the parents would want to learn the *Peace Process*, too. They could teach their parents how to do it also. Of course, doing retreats is another way to open minds to the possibilities." Kim smiled.

"Maybe summer camps for children," Christine proposed.

"Absolutely, that would be wonderful because they would be in a natural setting. All they need to do is appreciate the beauty and focus on peace. Let's visualize this being in all the schools in ten years." Kim suggested.

"Well, let's do that. Let's visualize the *Peace Process* taught in all the schools in ten years, helping children develop respect for themselves and their parents. We will see kids that are forgiving and centered in love," Christine said with enthusiasm.

"I think it is important that children learn to forgive." Kim nodded.

"And to accept what is, which is love," Christine added.

"Yes—that each person, each child is already perfect!" Kim declared.

"That's right. Even though each child is unique, they can come together in peace."

"This process lends itself to being taught at a church or a youth group."

"Mmm, right," Christine agreed.

"There are so many possibilities." Kim smiled.

"Jesus taught his disciples to extend love—no matter what. So, let's give credit where credit is due. Jesus demonstrated forgiveness, which is an important thought—and now it's a process, the *Peace Process*. We can teach and model forgiveness within ourselves," Christine reflected.

"This is off the track a little bit, but it is an interesting story. There is a little girl at my girls' school that hits people all the time. She has a lot of anger and she takes it out on the other children. One day, my children came home and asked what they could do because she hits them—she hits everybody. When I went on a field trip with their class, she was in my group. I told my children to treat her with kindness—always be nice to her. And, by the end of the field trip she was playing with the other children and finally making friends. She saw the kindness, and it brought a smile to her face," Kim recalled.

"They gave up the fear that she would hit them—and they were nice to her instead."

"Exactly. They turned their attitude around, and she turned hers around." Kim nodded.

"Isn't it amazing that we tend to get what we expect?" Christine was delighted at Kim's insight.

"Absolutely, and that's what we need to teach," Kim confirmed.

"So, if we expect peace, and we make the effort toward peace, then peace will come. Peace is simply a by-product of sending love." Christine paused. "Thank you, Kim."

"You're welcome." Kim smiled. "Thank you, Christine. This has been a profound experience—something that will live with me forever."

"Kim, there are butterflies floating around the tree behind you. So, we know you've been transformed," Christine laughed.

"I've shed my cocoon," Kim said lightly.

"Exactly," Christine agreed.

"And, spread my wings." Kim smiled.

"Thank you, God," Christine said gratefully.

"Thank you." Kim said once more as Christine turned off the video camera.

10.9 EXERCISE

1. Where do you spend most of your time and energy?

2. What causes you the most stress?

3. How can you adjust your environment to help balance your mind, body, and spirit?

EPILOGUE

"You should go to your piano lesson," Tom encouraged me. I hesitated to respond as I looked out the front window through the rain at the withered oaks swaying in the high wind.

"Okay I'll go," I decided.

"Drive carefully." Tom's voice floated down from his office upstairs.

"I will, honey. I'll stop at the grocery store on the way home. Love you!" I said goodbye and left in the downpour.

Due to the weather, I arrived a few minutes late at Penny's house in Indian Harbour Beach. It wasn't raining when I got out of the car, shut the door, and walked past the iron horse head on a post that marked the red brick entrance. Without knocking, I opened the door with my piano book and glasses in hand.

"Hi Penny!" I called out. Even though I couldn't see her, I sensed that she was close. Sometimes Penny would be checking a casserole in the oven, or fussing over baby Reece, her three-month old granddaughter.

"I'm here! I'll be right there!" Penny called back from the kitchen. In a moment, she popped out from the kitchen doorway. "Baby Reece is gone," her face twisted into a sad expression. "Her daddy picked her up early today."

"Aw." I smiled sympathetically. Penny retired this year, after twenty-seven years as a music teacher in public school.

"Well, what did you play this week?" Penny sat down in the antique chair next to her grandfather's Steinway.

"*Dangerous Journey*." I coaxed the bench in a few inches until my right foot was comfortable on the pedal. "Ever since I heard Michael play it at the recital, I thought it was a great piece." My fingers found the position to begin and I played the rest from memory. There were no words to the tune, but there was a pattern that my fingers followed, like a waterfall down the keyboard.

"Very good," Penny nodded. "It seems that you are playing everything better the second time around. Did you play *Moonlight* this week?"

"Maybe once. I'll play that for you before I go," I promised. Penny's Siamese cat hopped on the piano bench. Boris curled up next to me as I stroked his luxurious fur coat.

"What are you going to practice for next week?" Penny thumbed through the next song in my notebook. "*A Whole New World*—we haven't done that one before, have we? It's long—seven pages. Let's not start that this week. Why don't you review from the beginning of your book?"

"Good idea," I agreed. "I leave for a conference in Newark, New Jersey on Thursday, and I won't be home until late on Sunday. I won't have much time to practice." I played *Moonlight Sonata* and said goodbye to Penny and her next piano student Carol, who sat on the couch next to Boris' Siamese sibling.

The next day, I made a connection between the seven pages of *A Whole New World* and the seven disciplines of the new Peace Consciousness. My vision of the peace symbol on August 5, 2000 is significant because this date adds 8 + 5 + 2000 to 2013 and points to a graduation, celebration, and commencement for a new era of peace for humanity.

A Whole New World would not happen by accident, I was sure of that. My piano teacher suggested I review from the beginning of my book—and I realized another assignment to study the nineteen binders of my handwritten journal that began on January 17, 1997. Eleven years later, on January 30, 2008, the material was complete. *The Christine Revelation* represents an agreement, a pledge, and a promise to share ancient wisdom and cosmic knowledge.

A Whole New World? No, Penny—we haven't done that one before! It will be a long process to awaken humanity and bring peace to every mind. *A Whole New World* would not start this week. The quirky universe was sending me to NEW ARK and I understood that the covenant for *A Whole New World* would be coming soon as the second book in the trilogy. *The Peace Prophecy: Star Child* maps consciousness onto the constellation Orion—the son of man in the sky—and delivers a message about the heavenly origin of humanity.

THE PEACE PROPHECY

The first in the trilogy, *The Peace Prophecy: Vision 2013*, introduces three methods to promote an awakening in human potential: Peace BEE, the *Peace Process*, and the new Peace Consciousness.

Six-Discipline Model

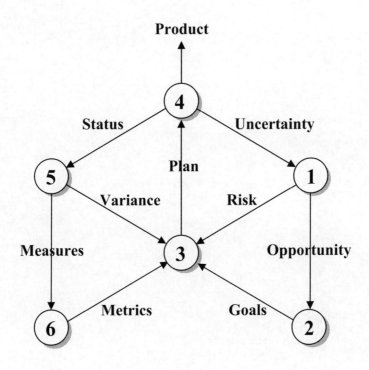

1. **Discover** the possibilities
2. **Envision** the product
3. **Plan** the work
4. **Work** the plan
5. **Measure** the work
6. **Value** the measures

6D Scientific Method

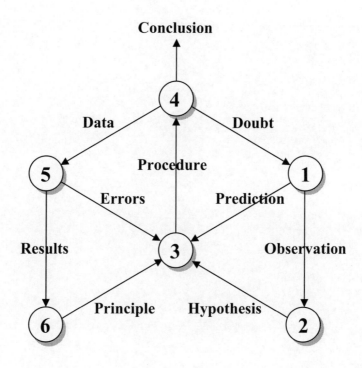

1. **Discover** by observation
2. **Envision** the hypothesis
3. **Plan** the procedure
4. **Work** the procedure
5. **Measure** the data
6. **Value** the results

The Peace Process

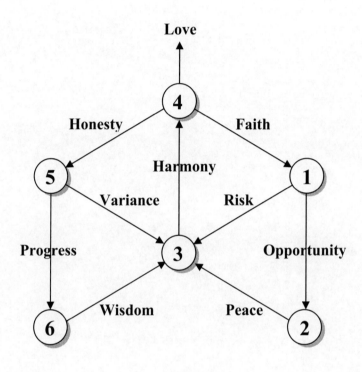

1. **Discover** the problem
2. **Envision** the solution
3. **Plan** for peace
4. **Work** for harmony
5. **Measure** the love
6. **Value** the progress

Peace Process Worksheet

(1) *Discover* the problem _____

_____

_____

(2) *Envision* the solution _____

_____

_____

(3) *Plan* for peace _____

_____

_____

(4) *Work* for harmony_____

_____

_____

(5) *Measure* the love_____

_____

_____

(6) *Value* the progress_____

_____

_____

KI-LIME: The Whole Pi

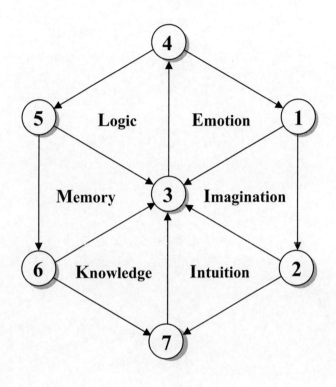

1. Discover
2. Envision
3. Plan
4. Work
5. Measure
6. Value
7. Energy

KfLlME: The Whole "P"

Logic

Memory Imagination

Knowledge Intuition

1. Discover
2. Revision
3. Plan
4. Work
5. Measure
6. Value
7. Manage

Peace Consciousness

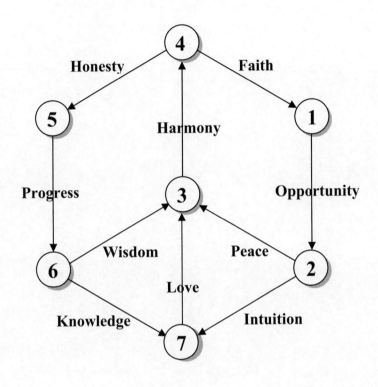

1. **Discover** the opportunity
2. **Envision** the peace
3. **Plan** with love
4. **Work** for harmony
5. **Measure** with honesty
6. **Value** the progress
7. **Energy** at rest

Harmonic Concordance

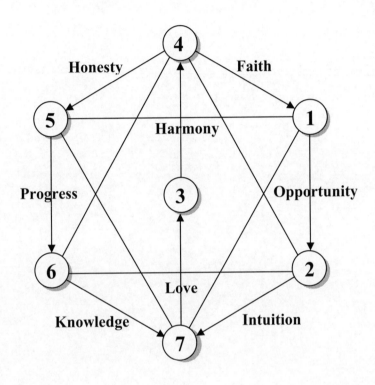

1. **Chiron** in Capricorn
2. **Mars** in Pisces
3. **Plan(et)** in Peace
4. **Sun** in Scorpio
5. **Jupiter** in Virgo
6. **Saturn** in Cancer
7. **Moon** in Taurus

I HOME

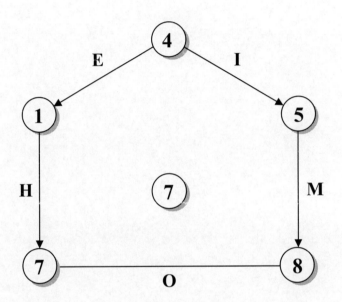

1. *Discover* (41/**5**)
2. *Envision* (44/**8**)
3. *Plan* (16/**7**)
4. *Work* (22/**4**)
5. *Measure* (28/10/**1**)
6. *Value* (16/**7**)

FIJI HOME

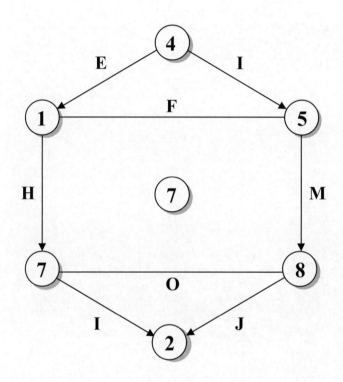

1. *Discover* (41/**5**)
2. *Envision* (44/**8**)
3. *Plan* (16/**7**)
4. *Work* (22/**4**)
5. *Measure* (28/10/**1**)
6. *Value* (16/**7**)
7. *Energy* (38/11/**2**)

THE CHALICE

Peace lives in harmony.

Love lives in peace.

God lives in love.

I live in God.

I love God.

I love

God.

God is in creation.

Love is in eternity.

In space, there is peace.

In time, there is harmony.

PEACE PROCESS TESTIMONIAL

"Last year I was demoted from a high-profile job to a fraction of my position at work. This event left me feeling resentful and depressed. My self-esteem plummeted while I allowed the past to weigh on me. I felt a sense of urgency to find a new job, one that reflected the financial security and recognition I had attained in my previous position. However, my ego had been scarred so that I was unable to attract a healthy work situation. I obviously had something to learn from this experience, and I needed time for this lesson to unfold.

Christine noticed my struggling and offered help in the form of her Peace Process. We spent a little over an hour one morning as she led me through steps to healing. I recall identifying the conflict, observing my feelings, visualizing my boss, and sending love and forgiveness to him and myself. I'm sure there were other components to Christine's model. I responded to each of her inquiries honestly and thoughtfully. When our session concluded, I felt more at peace with my sense of self and my situation.

This experience became profound, however, one or two days after participating in the Peace Process. Something had certainly shifted. I had called my corporate office to speak with a co-worker. While we were on the line, our boss asked to speak with me for the first time in several months.

His words were so comforting and genuine. He praised my recent work on a project, and let me know that my demotion was not a reflection of my past experience at the company, but rather based on one situation that had uncontrollable circumstances. Just hearing his affirming words is what I needed to move on and to heal from this incident.

Once I had this conversation, I was able to truly let go of the negative self-talk and beliefs that I had adopted since my demotion. I believe that I would not have had the same conversation had I not come to peace with the situation beforehand.

Thank you, Christine for sharing your Peace Process with me. It literally worked overnight!"

—Gretchen North, W. Harrison, New York

Join the Christine Community

Have you ever been invited to a wedding? Something old, something new, something borrowed, something blue. Ah, weddings—a joyful celebration of love! With vows to love in good times and bad, in sickness and in health, the Christine Community is like a sacred marriage that soothes your soul.

A nationwide network of women guided by spiritual ideals of peace and love, the Christine Community uplifts humanity by helping those who cry out for emotional understanding, awareness, and inner peace. We are called to divine service as educators, teachers, counselors, ministers, chaplains, elders, therapists, psychologists, doctors, nurses, social workers, and humanitarians. Our purpose is peace. Our vision is simple: *Peace to Every Mind.*®

We offer mentored group study online, and provide training and certification for *Peace Process* facilitators. I invite you to learn about the resources and support available for your spiritual growth. Please join us at **www.thepeaceprophecy.com**.